CORVETTE

·T·H·E·

Enduring Legend

Text and photography by

NICKY WRIGHT

CORVETTE

·T·H·E·

Enduring Legend

GALLERY BOOKS
An Imprint of W. H. Smith Publishers Inc.
112 Madison Avenue
New York City 10016

DEDICATION

This book is dedicated to Roger and David Judski of Roger's Corvette Center, Orlando, Florida, and the National Corvette Restorers Society. Without the help of Roger and David and NCRS members across Florida and the South, this book would not have been possible. My grateful thanks.

ACKNOWLEDGEMENT

The author gratefully acknowledges the invaluable assistance provided by the following individuals and organizations throughout the preparation of this book:
Brent Ferguson; Roger Judski; David Judski; Fran and Mike Westrich; Nancy Libby, Chevrolet Public Relations; Kari St. Antoine, Chevrolet Public Relations; Chevrolet Motor Division; Cypress Gardens, Florida; Dan Gale; Bill Locke; Ed Augustine; Tom Edwards, JH Associates, New York; Vette Vues Magazine; Bob Rush; Lois and Dennis Stradtman; Robbie Tucker; Henry Choate; George M. Augustine; Patti and Joseph Linzalone; Dr. Ernie Hendry; Bobby Allen; Jeff Joyner; Sam Feinman/Gregory Genco; Michael J. Foldi; special thanks to Rod Butler and Kenn JeSchonek.

DESIGNED BY DICK RICHARDSON
EDITED BY JOHN PHILLIPS

CLB 2354

This edition published in 1991 by Gallery Books,
an imprint of W.H. Smith Publishers, Inc.,
112 Madison Avenue, New York 10016.
Printed and bound in Hong Kong.
ISBN 0 8317 1782 3

Gallery Books are available for bulk purchase for sales promotions and premium use. For details write or telephone
the Manager of Special Sales, W.H. Smith Publishers, Inc,
112 Madison Avenue, New York, New York 10016 (212) 532-6600.

INTRODUCTION

When we think of sports cars our thoughts turn to Europe – to Britain, France, Germany and Italy. Visions of fleet Jaguars, charismatic MGs and wondrous Ferraris cross our minds. Ah, we might say to ourselves, those are the cars from which legends are made, tales of man and machine are told. But wait a minute! Haven't we forgotten something? What about America? What about the Corvette?

Europeans laughed when General Motors' Chevrolet Division unveiled the Corvette. It had a white plastic body, red interior, Chevrolet's antiquated Blue Flame Six under the hood and, would you believe, a two-speed automatic transmission! Three-legged turtles out of water would go faster. Italians shook their heads and turned back to their Alfas and Maseratis. The English? Well, the English had not thought much of American cars since the war, labelling Detroit's efforts as too big, too chrome-laden and too wallowy. "The Corvette? That's no sports car," they cried. "That's just another Chevrolet with a flashy body."

In a sense they were right, for under its plastic skin the Corvette was essentially a Bel-Air. As we shall see, though, there were essential differences not shared with America's then most popular car. After the 1953 Motorama Show Car received such an enthusiastic response from the public, Corvette production began on the last day of June 1953.

Public enthusiasm has gone overboard before at Motorama shows. But once it is all over and the people return to the house payments, the telephone bill and the infant who needs a swing set in the garden, they tend to forget Show cars. As the Corvette took its first hesitant roll out of Chevrolet's Flint, Michigan, plant, many corporate heads regarded it as a seven-day wonder.

Thankfully they were wrong. The seven-day wonder is alive, well and prospering thirty-eight years later. It almost wasn't though. GM management expected to sell at least 20,000 Corvettes a year, but by the end of 1954 the actual 3,600 production figure was way off target. Magazines like *Road & Track* were patient with the funny little plastic car; they even liked it. And others were more generous with their praise. But in GM's corporate ivory towers there was talk of killing it off before 1955. Then fate stepped in and worked a couple of "divine" miracles.

First was the news that Ford was bringing out a very stylish V-8 powered two-seater in 1955; second was Chevrolet's brand new 1955 V-8 engine, and third was engineer Zora Arkus-Duntov. The upshot was a revitalized Corvette for 1955, powered by Chevy's new V-8. It was a 100 percent improvement and Corvette was here to stay.

Corvette rocketed to the forefront of sports car technology in 1957 with better handling and the headlining fuel injection system, courtesy the legendary Corvette engineer Zora Arkus-Duntov. With fuel injection Chevrolet boasted 283 hp from 283 cubic inches, although 290 horsepower was nearer the truth.

From 1955 to 1990 Corvette has not looked back. Fuel injection arrived in 1957 and engineer Duntov was working miracles. He built the racing SS Corvette and it was entered for the Sebring 12 Hour Race. The car retired after twenty-three laps, mainly due to the limited time that had been available for development. Then, before Chevrolet could go further, the Automobile Manufacturers' Association issued its damaging edict regarding competition and the gray men at GM ordered a complete stop to all sporting activity.

None of this prevented Corvette going from strength to strength in the marketplace. By 1960 the world realized that Corvette was not some flash-in-the-pan gimmick, and the Europeans had stopped laughing. Then came the legendary Duntov-engineered, Bill Mitchell-designed 1963 Sting Ray. There were a few things not quite right with it, but the Sting Ray was right up there with the Europeans.

Big block V-8s with 427 cubic inches crammed under the hood made mid-sixties Corvettes the terrors of the turnpikes. Would you believe 0-60 in 4.7 seconds? Those were the days Corvette really cut its teeth and became a young man's dream, the King of the Road. On TV the popular road series *Route 66* became a cult and turned a trio into stars. The two young actors have long since evaporated into the mists of time, but the Corvette will always be remembered.

In the late sixties came a new generation of Corvettes to greet the emissions-cloudy seventies. Where had all the flowers gone? A decade of dullness; a nation trying to find itself. Through soul-searching and inflation, Chevrolet kept on improving, making its sports car – America's only sports car – a world class piece of machinery.

With the arrival of 1981 Corvette production moved from St. Louis to a brand new, state-of-the-art factory at Bowling Green, Kentucky. The upshot of that move was the 1984 Corvette. It was the first really new Corvette for fifteen years. Its svelte good looks were augmented by the latest engineering technology. Handling was on a par with the very best Europe could offer. But improved handling was achieved at the cost of comfort and complaints were loud and long.

We are now into the last decade of the 20th century. Corvette has become a respected name across the globe, and people stand in line for the world-class 189 mph ZR-1. Chevrolet's little plastic baby has grown up to become a world beater; a car with handling and comfort to match. Yes, Corvette engineers cured the 1984 problems. Ranked among the world's best sports cars and still the only one made in America, the Corvette story is fascinating and fun. Due to space limitations I have been unable to detail a comprehensive history, but I hope that what you read here will encourage further investigation of this great and glorious sports car.

Though many favor the 1963 split rear window design, the 1967 Corvette Sting Ray was by far the cleanest of the four-year body styles. It was also the most potent, with the massive 427-cubic-inch V8 delivering 435 bhp in its top state of tune. Red line tires were a popular sporty option in the mid Sixties.

CHAPTER ONE
A PRELUDE TO GREATNESS

From the very beginning, America and Europe viewed the automobile in quite different ways. For the English and Germans, French and Italians, the fledgling horseless carriage was a plaything for the wealthy, a motorized toy to go gadding about in. For most of Europe's people there existed a chasm – a chasm called class. On one side played the rich; on the other, starved the poor. And motorcars were meant only for those born with a silver spoon, a mansion on the hill and holdings in Africa.

In America it was different. There was no class in this unruly land. Money didn't come from daddy's trust fund: it came from honest hard work. Everybody could own an automobile in America if they were able to afford it. The car was a means to an end. To ensure everyone could own a car Henry Ford created the Model T, and financial institutions were only too happy to loan the money to prospective buyers, offering installment terms that would suit even the less well-off.

How times have changed. In some European countries class was the precursor to bloody revolution. In others the social climate changed drastically. By the mid-twenties a strong middle-class had come into being, fuelled by the events of the Great War and changing attitudes of the establishment. Little Austin Sevens and Citroëns became the order of the day. Though moderated by circumstance, the wealthy were still wealthy, and Mercedes. Rolls, Packard and Bentley were their proverbial cup of tea.

If you have money you have time to have fun, and this can take many forms, depending on what you like. Some like gentle pursuits such as playing croquet; for others their escape is adventure, danger, thrills, such as motor racing and fast cars. Which is how the sports car first came into being. Machines capable of high turns of speed tickled many imaginations and fuelled competitive desires. Soon sports cars, mostly expensive sports cars, came flooding out of the factories: Bentley, Bugatti, Mercedes, Napier.

In America during the early part of the century, the idea of fast, sporty automobiles had been encouraged by tales of derring-do on the other side of the Atlantic. It wasn't long before Stutz and Mercer discovered that placing a cut-down, lightweight body on top of a good chassis and powerful engine resulted in speed and performance: a sports car, in other words. Mercer had the Raceabout, Stutz the Bearcat. Neither lasted any length of time however, and it appeared that America's honeymoon with the sports car was over. Far better to churn out comfortable carriages able to take people cross-country in style and splendor.

1953-55
SPECIFICATIONS

Engine: Ohv six-cylinder inline (1953-55) ohv V-8 (1955). Water-cooled; cast-iron block and head. Bore and stroke: 3.56 x 3.95/3.75 x 3.00 ins. Bhp: 150 @ 4200/195 @ 5000. Compression ratio: 8.0:1/8.0:1. Carburetion: 3 Carter sidedraft/1 Carter 4-barrel.
Chassis: Front suspension: Independent upper and lower A-arms, coil springs, anti-roll bar, tubular hydraulic shock absorbers. Rear suspension: Live axle on semi-elliptic leaf springs, tubular hydraulic shock absorbers. Steering: Saginaw worm-and-sector, 16:1 ratio, 3.7 turns lock-to-lock. Brakes: 4-wheel hydraulic, internal-expanding drums, 11-in. dia.; 154.5 sq. ins. effective lining area. Transmission: 2-speed Powerglide torque-converter automatic (3-speed manual fitted to a few late '55 models). Final drive ratio: 3,55:1.
Measurements: Weight: 2980lbs. Tire size: 6.70 x 15 4-ply whitewalls. Track: 57.0 front, 59.0 rear. Wheelbase: 102.0" Overall length: 167.0" Overall width: 72.2" Overall height: 51.3" Maximum speed: 107/120mph. Fuel consumptiom: 14-18mpg or 18-22.5mpg.

Top left: provided it isn't profane, you can choose what you want for your license plate. The owner of this splendid 1953 chose to celebrate the fact that his car was the last off the line before the switch to 1954 models. Only 300 were built in 1953 and the car featured here is number 300. Even though the Corvette was hardly sporting, it certainly looked the part (facing page top), with stone guards (top) protecting the headlights from damage. One reason for its lack of sporting prowess was Chevy's old "stovebolt six" (facing page bottom) and a two-speed Powerglide transmission.

Sports cars didn't die entirely, though. While Cecil Kimber was busy cutting up Morris cars to make the first MGs, and William Lyons was toying with the idea of building more than just another customized Austin, individual Americans with mechanical ability were creating their own sports cars. These became known as hot rods, cars made up from Model Ts, Model As, chopped and channeled, a big engine in the opening once covered by a hood. Apart from speedy, and generally expensive, grand tourers such as Dusenberg SJs or the far less pricey Auburn Supercharged Boat-tail Speedster, the sports car was dead in America.

With the advent of the Second World War American troops, sent to play their part in defeating Hitler, discovered the sports car again. Either pre-war Mercedes SSKs confiscated from German officers or the pretty little MG TA that belonged to the veterinarian's pretty daughter in the pretty little English town. Americans were sold. Particularly on MGs. There was nothing like it back home. Why, you'd be the king on your street with one of these! The love affair continues to this day.

By 1950 America's motor industry was working double time to keep up with the demand for new cars. Big cars, chrome-laden cars, cars painted all colors of the rainbow. Unwieldy at the crossroads and uncontrollable in fast bends perhaps, but never mind the deficiencies: they looked good, they were comfortable and they sold like hot cakes. So too, though in numbers Detroit would regard as a drop in the ocean, did European sports cars. Although MG and Jaguar factories were working flat-out they couldn't hope to satisfy the demand for sports cars that had been created by returning GIs.

Harley Earl had been with GM since 1927 and had formed the Art and Color Design Studio, the first of its kind simply to create automobile styling. Here he was, twenty-three years later, GM vice-president of styling. He had been responsible for most of GM's designs since 1927, if not personally, then certainly as the chief of the Art and Color Studio. If he liked something one of his stylists had rendered, he would give it his blessing. Of course, the studio stylist never received recognition; Harley Earl was the man who was applauded. This is common practice in the motor industry; it is always the chief who gets the credit for something one of his staff may have done. That, unfortunately, is life in this unfair world.

Nevertheless, Harley Earl was a man of great talent and keen mind. Unlike some of the men in his position, he liked to get back to the drawing board, scribble ideas and discuss them with members of his staff. He kept a small, walled-off area near the main studio where he would talk over ideas and work on future projects before higher management caught wind of them. Considering Earl's work revolved round full-size six-passenger vehicles with oodles of chrome, it seemed hardly likely that he would be interested in anything like a sports car.

But he was.

It was 1951 and Harley Earl went down to his alcove and started doodling. Always the force behind the lavish Motorama "Dream Cars," his latest, the swish Buick LeSabre replete with tailfins and panoramic wraparound windshield, was wowing spectators at Motoramas across the country. Most of his recent show cars had sporty, two-seater interiors,

Corvette was always an attractive car, even if the fiberglass panels didn't fit as well as they might. The 1955 model looked much like those of the previous two years, but the big news was the much-needed inclusion of Ed Cole's sparkling new Chevrolet V8. Rated at 195 bhp, the V8 turned an also-ran into a serious sports car, and the Corvette hasn't looked back since.

24

but they were far too long to be considered a match for European makes. Earl kept thinking it was time for an American-made sports car.

Earl's first thoughts were influenced by British sports cars and, of all things, the Willys Jeepster. What he had in mind was something simple and relatively cheap – about $1,850, the sort of price the very popular MG TD was fetching. The first seeds of the Corvette were being sown.

About the time Harley Earl was thinking of his sports car, a brilliant engineer by the name of Edward N. Cole was transferred from Cadillac to become Chief Engineer of the Chevrolet Division. It was as if Fate had decreed Cole's transfer, for he was to become one of the major architects behind the Corvette. One of the first things he did was to triple Chevrolet's engineering staff and set to work on designing a new engine for Chevrolet (this engine would be the legendary ohv V-8 launched in 1955).

While Earl was becoming serious about his sports car and Cole was shaping his Chevrolet seat to fit, GM was showing off the oddly named "Alembic 1" in its Styling Auditorium. The Alembic 1 was a styling study for the U.S. Rubber Company from a design by Bill Tritt. U.S. Rubber

then loaned it to GM, which resulted in Harley Earl being further motivated to work on his sports car.

First he took aside a fresh young designer named Robert F. McLean, who came to GM Styling with an armful of degrees and an interest in sports cars, and asked him to provide the basis for what was now officially termed "Project Opel". Why Opel? Because Chevrolet was known to do advanced studies for GM's German subsidiary. Using Opel as a code name would act like a red herring; rival parties would associate any goings-on with Opel.

McLean had never designed a whole car before, but here he was with a clean sheet of paper in his hands and a personal directive from the king of stylists to come up with a sharp-looking sports car. As he was beginning to put pen to paper, Harley Earl was looking into the feasibility of producing his car out of plastic. There was a lot of talk around Motown about a revolutionary new material called glass-reinforced plastic. It was extremely durable, never rusted and was cheap to produce. Chevrolet built a Bel-Air convertible body out of GRP, and what finally convinced Earl that fiberglass was a better material to use than steel was the report that, during high-speed testing at GM's proving grounds, the driver flipped the plastic bodied Bel-Air and walked away unhurt. As for the car, it was hardly damaged.

At the design studio, McLean was working hard on the design that would eventually become the Corvette. Instead of using conventional designers' methods – that is starting from the firewall and working round it – McLean began at the rear axle and worked forwards. The result was a car with a 102-inch wheelbase, a long hood, a passenger compartment set as close to the rear axle as possible, and an engine set seven inches further back in the chassis than would be considered normal at the time. The goal had been a 50/50 weight distribution for good handling; in the end it didn't quite work out, but a 53/47 percent split was a great achievement.

By 1952 Harley Earl and Ed Cole had sold the idea of a fiberglass sports car to Chevrolet General Manager Thomas Keating and GM President Harlow Curtice. Now the race was on to have a prototype ready for the first 1953 Motorama Show at New York's plush Waldorf-Astoria.

To keep production costs to the minimum, the Corvette was to be built around as many stock Chevrolet components as possible. There had been talk of using Chevrolet's chassis, but this idea was dropped because

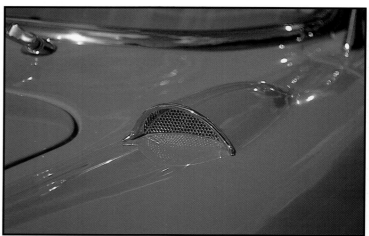

The 1957 Corvette was the same as 1956 but sported more conventional headlights (top), with dummy scoops (above) perched atop the front fenders. These were supposed to be functional, but costs ruled that out. Rocket ship taillight styling was replaced by recessed units (facing page top), and the script above the attractive emblem (facing page bottom) let you know what this car was supposed to be all about.

28

McLean's engine positioning called for a new design. Using boxed side-members for additional strength, the X-member chassis was given a solid rear axle and leaf springs. At the front was the independent coil-over arrangement of Englishman Maurice Olley, the ex-Rolls Royce engineer. Olley, by the way, had developed GM's knee-action independent front suspension in 1934 and was probably responsible for teaching Americans all they knew about the subject at that time. The frame's front crossmember was from the Chevy parts bin, as was the bolt-on sub-assembly, used by Chevrolet since 1934.

As for the engine, there was no choice other than Chevrolet's dependable ohv Blue Flame Six. The V-8 was still two years away, so Ed Cole had to do something with the existing motor, which had started out in the mid-twenties. Developed by Ormond E. Hunt, this reliable powerplant was refined and honed to near perfection as a solid, indestructible engine that would power millions of Chevrolet cars and trucks for almost thirty years. Now its ultimate test was at hand as the engine for America's first production sports car.

In standard guise the Blue Flame produced 105 hp, not earth-shattering for a 1953 sports car that Harley Earl confidently predicted would take away most of the sales from MG and Jaguar. To give the engine a better showing, Ed Cole modified the head to give an 8.0:1 compression ratio (stock engines were 7.5:1). A major alteration came with the inclusion of triple Carter "YH" side-draft carburetors. This alone made a world of difference. Each carburetor fed a pair of cylinders and they all worked in unison via a manual choke. Automatic chokes couldn't be synchronized, so production cars were fitted with the manual one. With the various alterations the engine's horsepower was now rated at 150, quite a jump from the standard unit.

An inch smaller diameter steering wheel than that used in basic Chevrolets was adopted for the Corvette, but the system was basic GM Saginaw recirculating ball with a quicker 16:1 ratio. The transmission was definitely strange; for some reason the engineers used Chevy's two-speed Powerglide. The excuse was that the engineers didn't believe they had a manual system strong enough to cope with the increased power the engine put out. The final touches were implemented on the Corvette Motorama show car in November 1952.

January 1953 and the curtain rose on the special podium that was part of Chevrolet's Motorama exhibit at the Wardorf-Astoria Hotel in New York. A hush, then an almighty cheer greeted the gleaming white two-seater sports car with bright red interior as it introduced itself to the world. The dreams of Harley Earl, Robert McLean and Ed Cole had come true: the Corvette was born.

Previous pages: the Corvette in profile is a handsome car ... this is another 1957 example. Note the recessed "coves" on the sides of the car; these were mostly in a contrasting color to the rest of the bodywork. From the angle shown right, the shaping of the "cove" looks awkward around the wheel arch. Performance was excellent with the fuel-injected engine, and zero to sixty could be reached in 5.9 seconds.

CHAPTER TWO
BELIEF IN A DREAM GOES A LONG WAY

The response to the Motorama Corvette was overwhelming. Everybody loved America's first true sports car, loved it more, probably, simply because it was built by Chevrolet. When is it coming out? Will I be able to order it through my Chevy dealer? – the questions about the car's availability started early in the morning and didn't finish until the show closed at night. This was sufficient inducement for Chevrolet, who decided to begin production as soon as possible.

On June 30th, 1953 production began at a small plant adjacent to Chevrolet's main factory in Flint, Michigan (the home of Buick, incidentally). Figures of 10,000 units had been talked about for 1954, but Chevrolet decreed that no more than 300 could be built during 1953, and as for 1954, well, they'd just have to wait and see....

Although Harley Earl liked the idea of using fiberglass, the powers-that-be weren't quite so sure. After all, fiberglass manufacture was still in its infancy. Would it not be safer to stick with steel? Proponents of fiberglass argued that the Corvette's rounded shapes might be expensive to stamp out in steel. However, a new lightweight metal called Kirksite was being seriously considered for possible use. One advantage was cost, but a major disadvantage was Kirksite's short lifespan. No decision was reached, and as the proposed production date drew closer Chevrolet put on the pressure, worried lest the Corvette schedules could not be met. Finally, after much discussion, the decision was made in favor of fiberglass. GM's premier division cited

1956-57
SPECIFICATIONS

Engine: Ohv 90-degree V-8, water-cooled, cast-iron block and head. Bore and stroke: 3.75 x 3.00; 3.875ins. Bhp: 210 @ 5600/240 @ 5200. 220 @ 4800/283 @ 6200. Compression ratio: 9.25/9.5:1 9.5/10.5:1. Carburetion: 1 or 24-barrel Rochester carbureter. Ramjet continuous-flow fuel injection (1957 only).
Chassis: Front suspension: Independent; unequal-length A-arms, coil springs, tubular hydraulic shock absorbers, anti-roll bar. Rear suspension: Live axle on semi-elliptic leaf springs, anti-roll bar, tubular hydraulic shock absorbers. Steering: Saginaw worm-and-ball, 16:1 ratio. Brakes: 4-wheel hydraulic, internal-expanding drums, 11-in. dia.; 157 sq. in. effective lining area. (121 sq. in. with optional sintered-metallic linings). Transmission: 3-speed manual, 4-speed manual (late 1957 only). 2-speed Powerglide automatic. Final drive ratio: 3.70:1 (4.56, 4.11, and 3.55 optional).
Measurements: Weight: 2730-2850lbs. Tire size: 6.70 x 15 4-ply. Track: 57.0 front, 59.0 rear. Wheelbase: 102.0" Overall length: 168.0" Overall width: 70.5" Overall height: 51.9" Maximum speed: 121-135mph. Fuel consumption: 10-16mpg.

Top: interior layout changed little in Corvette's early years and was Spartan compared with what Americans were generally used to. Facing page top: whichever way one looks at it, the 1957 Corvette is a strikingly handsome car complete with sporty accessories such as tachometer (facing page bottom). Dropped after 1955 were the awkward side curtains; conventional roll-up windows came in 1956 and remain to this day.

flexibility, low cost, damage resistance, paint compatibility and freedom from drumming noises as the reasons for the choice. The go-ahead was given and production got under way. Although Chevrolet told a few white lies about the advantages of fiberglass – early models and paint weren't exactly complementary, and the plastic bodies suffered from awful noise problems – it was right about the material's flexibility. A photograph was issued showing a fiberglass Corvette body broken down into nine major components, including the entire floorpan, from trunk to firewall. A picture showing a man holding the floorpan above his head with one hand demonstrated the weight advantages of the material.

Counting all the minor parts that had to be attached, a Corvette body consisted of forty-six separate pieces, far fewer than a comparable steel car. Logic tells us that a car with so few pieces should be simple to build. Anyone who has ever attempted to build a car using a fiberglass kit, however, will be keenly aware of the problems involved. While instructions may claim that it will take only TWO weekends to finish the job, what is not mentioned is that a degree in fiberglass assembly and another in engineering are required. Six months later a half-finished car, one fender higher than the other and a hood that won't shut is offered in the local Peddlers' Post. Well, at Corvette's plant it was rather like that in the beginning.

Fortunately, though, Chevrolet persevered. Even with all the problems and the lack of experience in fiberglass production, the 315 cars manufactured in 1953 were quite remarkable. Ill-fitting panels, undulating body surfaces, paint that didn't stay (and if it did, it wasn't for long), and body resonance that drowned out any attempt at conversation all came as standard. There were no side windows, either. In keeping with what was considered European tradition, the Corvette came with side curtains.

Of course, all the auto magazines wanted to get their hands on the car. And when they did, most had favorable comments about the Corvette. Both *Motor Trend* and the hyper-critical *Road and Track* praised the car's looks, ride and handling. As for performance, the Corvette could hold its own against most European sports cars, but some, like Jaguar, would leave it gasping in their exhaust. Still, a 0–60 time of about 11 seconds, combined with a 106 mph top speed, wasn't bad for the car's admittedly antiquated engine.

At the end of 1953 production was moved to Chevrolet's facility at St. Louis, Missouri, where, according to the ever-optimistic Chevrolet PR department, production would reach 1,000 units a month. Not quite. By year's end, only 3,640 1954 Corvettes had been built and Chevrolet found itself stuck with a surplus of 1,500 unsold. On the face of it, the future didn't bode well for Corvette.

Once again, just as it had with Harley Earl, fate took a kindly and extremely important hand. Zora Arkus-Duntov, a Belgian-born Russian, had trained in engineering in Germany and had worked with English car maker Sidney Allard for a while. He was responsible for the design and development of the ARDUN cylinder head which was used to convert flathead Ford V-8s into a hot-rodder's dream. Not long after Ed Cole became chief engineer at Chevrolet, Duntov sent him a paper describing high-performance engines. Cole was impressed, and in May 1953 Duntov

Many Corvette enthusiasts weren't too happy when the face-lifted 1958 model appeared. Styling was basically the same, but with added glitz. The chrome grin now sported nine "teeth" instead of thirteen, and dummy side scoops and hood louvers were add-ons. The model shown is a 1959 convertible. Note no fake louvers; obviously the stylists thought the car looked better without them.

started work at Chevrolet's Research and Development department, where he soon became involved in Corvette's development.

Everybody was getting ready for 1955. This was going to be a banner year; everything new – new styling, new engines and new cars. New cars! The General received word that Ford was preparing a brand new model for 1955. It would be sleek, would have a V-8 engine as standard and, worst of all, it was going to be a two-seater. Suddenly the doubters who wanted to end the Corvette experiment in the closing months of 1954, changed their minds. If Ford was going to have a sporty car, then Chevrolet would certainly not make itself a laughing stock by dropping the Corvette.

The final deciding factor was Ed Cole's V-8. Slated for availability in all Chevy models for 1955, might it not be a good idea to cram it under the Corvette's hood? It was agreed, therefore, that the Corvette should have a stay of execution. If nothing else, the extra performance capabilities would be sure to attract attention. There were some annoying problems to overcome first, however. No one liked the dummy knock-off wheel covers for instance, or the manually operated top which refused to operate and was of very poor quality. Mechanically, the car was fine; that old Blue Flame Six would run for ever.

This was the year in which GM produced its fifty millionth car, a gold-painted sports coupé which dazzled the eye with its 600 gold-plated parts, One wonders where that car is now.

Anyone who knows anything about cars will know that 1955 was an incredible year – a banner year. Sales went through the roof and broke all records set since the first American car, the Duryea, tottered onto the road in 1893.

1958 SPECIFICATIONS

Engine: Ohv V-8, water-cooled, cast-iron block and head. Bore and stroke: 3.88 x 3.00ins. Bhp: 250 @ 5000. Compression ratio: 9.5:1 (10.5:1 with Duntov cam). Carburetion: Ramjet fuel injection.
Chassis: Front suspension: Independent; upper and lower A-arms, unequal-length wishbones, coil springs, tubular hydraulic shock absorbers. Steering: Saginaw recirculating-ball; 17:1 overall ratio, 3.7 turns lock-to-lock. Brakes: 4-wheel hydraulic, 11-in. dia.; internal expanding drums; 157 sq. in. effective lining area. Transmission: 3-speed manual, optional 2-speed Powerglide automatic. Final drive ratio: 3.70:1 (4.11:1, 4.56:1, 3.55:1 with Powerglide optional).
Measurements: Weight: 2912lbs. Tire size: 6.70 x 15 4-ply. Track: 57.0 front, 59.7 rear. Wheelbase: 102.0″ Overall length: 177.0″ Overall width: 73.0″ Overall height: 51.0″ Maximum speed: 125mph (est). Fuel consumption: 15-18mpg.

Top left: this 1959 car is fitted with the optional two-speed Powerglide transmission; most testers preferred the four-speed manual box. Equipped with the mildest 283 and Powerglide, a Corvette wouldn't win any races but was the best boulevard cruiser in town, nonetheless. Above: Corvette caught the twin headlight disease, a fad of the late Fifties, as can be seen here. Facing page: even though the front of the '59 was busy, the bumble bee rear was left alone. Note the exhaust outlets through the bumpers.

By year's end, over seven million cars had been sold and one-and-a-half million of them were Chevrolets. Of that one-and-a-half million, only 674 were Corvettes, and of these only six were ordered with the Blue Flame Six.

Everybody had V-8s for 1955 including not just Chevy of the low priced three, but Ford and Plymouth as well. (Ford always had V-8s and had changed to an ohv design in 1954.) Ed Cole's new 265-cubic-inch engine was regarded as a masterpiece then, and it remains a masterpiece now. Cole once said about his engine that it had to have five main bearings and a 265-cubic-inch displacement that would allow a 3.75 x 3.00-inch bore and stroke. "We released our engine for tooling direct from the drawing boards," Cole told *Special Interest Autos*. "That's how crazy and confident we were."

There was a little more to this engine than that. Unlike in some engines there was no common rocker shaft, so with each rocker arm working by itself the deflection of one had no effect on the others. The intake manifold had a common outlet for water to be delivered simultaneously to both heads. Even though the small block unit actually weighed less than the six, both heads were die-cast. But the slipper type pistons were aluminum and the crankshaft was pressed steel instead of iron.

Forty-three percent of all Chevrolet buyers ordered the new V-8, which developed either 162 or 180 hp depending on its state of tune. For the Corvette, though, the engine was given a special camshaft and a single Rochester four bbl carburetor – standard engines had a multiple carburetor arrangement. These modifications gave the Corvette 195 bhp at 5,000 rpm. Performance was vastly improved: 0-60 in 8.5 seconds and the engine only ran out of wind at 120 mph. This was not bad considering the wretched two-speed Powerglide was still the only available transmission until the end of the 1955 run when a few cars were fitted with a new three-speed close-ratio manual box.

Besides the exciting new engine, the Corvette received a few other improvements as well, including 12-volt electrics in common with other GM cars; the six sixes still retained the 6-volt system. Britain, incidentally, had been using 12-volt electrics since well before World War Two. American cars sold in Britain during the thirties were converted to 12 volts upon their arrival.

An automatic choke replaced the manual one used since 1953 and the antiquated vacuum windshield wiper motor was replaced by an electric unit. Another plus was improved workmanship, which steadily got better as faults were found and eliminated.

Although the 1955 Corvette was saved at the last minute, sales were dismal compared with all other makes, causing the cost accountants so much concern that they advocated stopping production of the model.

At Ford things were very different. The beautifully styled Thunderbird two-seater was selling well – compared to Corvette, extremely well. Over 16,000 of Ford's "personal" car – Ford never referred to the T-Bird as a sports car – were sold in 1955. This humiliation angered Chevrolet; the Number One automaker in the land was tiring of Ford's continuous

After eight years Corvette finally lost its distinctive teeth, which were replaced by a mesh grille in 1961. The standard 283 engine developed 230 bhp, but a fuel-injected 315 bhp version was an option. This powerhouse could move the Corvette to a respectable 130-mph-plus top speed with ease.

assaults on its superiority. Ford, impatient that Chevrolet had been No. 1 for more than twenty years, had declared war on its arch-rival in 1953 and was narrowing the gap considerably. Both sides purposely overstocked their dealerships, instructing them to sell no matter what. By the year's end Chevrolet pipped Ford, 1.5 million to 1.4 million.

The accountants were defeated. Management wanted to thrash Ford for its insolence and the Corvette was once again reprieved to do battle with the T-Bird. Apart from the much-needed V-8 there was very little else Chevrolet could do to encourage more sales of the 1955 Corvette. Harley Earl realized this too, and earlier that year he and his staff had been finalizing a new body for 1956. Criticisms of the 1953/55 models had been that the car was too effeminate and that it had become too luxury orientated. This was to change for 1956: Corvette was to get a more masculine image. It was going to become a real sports car.

Evolutionary rather than revolutionary would be the way to describe the 1956 Corvette restyle. Even so, the body looked a lot different with the exception of the wraparound windshield, the grille with its vertical bars and outer bumper appendages. Gone were the 1953/55 rocket-ship taillight extensions, to be replaced by concave shaped units fitting flush with the rear fenders. An artful and very attractive touch was the concave sweep that started at the rear of the front wheel-arch and ended just ahead, and below, the door handle. Painted a contrasting color to the rest of the car, this clever styling touch was reminiscent of the coachbuilt Dusenbergs and other such exotica of the thirties.

Meanwhile, Zora Arkus-Duntov had been busy rethinking the engine compartment. Never a man to mince words, he described his first impression of the 1953 Corvette as

"awful." In later interviews he recalled altering the suspension to give it a neutral stance, but in his own time, not on production models. One of his first assignments with the Corvette was to work on the exhaust outlets at the rear, the fashion trait at the time being that the exhaust emitted through the body. Because they were almost flush with the body, the area round the outlets discolored badly. Duntov simply extended the pipes six inches further out. End of problem.

Already equipped with one of the finest V-8 engines the world has ever seen, the 1956 Corvette only required a tweak here and there to boost its power. Duntov gave it that tweak. He designed a special camshaft which raised torque to 270 lbs/ft at 3,600 rpm. This, as any engineer will tell you, is quite impressive. Combined with a cast aluminum intake manifold and dual four bbl carburetors, the engine's horsepower was now 225 but could go to 240. The three-speed manual introduced very late in the 1955 model run had been improved and was standard. As for the Powerglide, that became a $189 option for those intent on boulevard cruising.

Top: the simulated reverse air extractor had been with Corvette since 1958 and wouldn't disappear until 1963, cleaning up the outline of the front wheel arch. Facing page top: the shape of things to come! The restyled deck was lifted directly from Bill Mitchell's Sting Ray racing car and integrated quite well with the overall design. Facing page bottom: grab handle and brushed aluminum insert add a nice touch to the interior.

SPLASH AREA

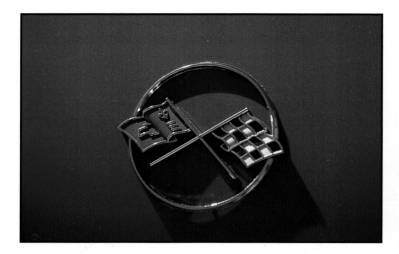

A 3.55:1 axle was standard, but a stronger 3.27:1 ratio could take the car close to 130 mph. Considering the skimpy tires of those days, Chevrolet offered wider wheels and high-speed tires, which were strongly recommended if the 3.27:1 ratio was used. With the standard axle 0-60 was accomplished in 7.3 seconds, according to one test, and the quarter mile, so important to Americans, in 15.8 seconds. This was with the 225-horsepower car, not the standard 210 bhp Corvette. So far, this model hasn't been mentioned, but there were two models for 1956. The 210-horsepower car had a single four-barrel carburetor but none of Duntov's "demons."

Karl Ludvigsen, one of the world's great automotive writers, tested the 225 hp Corvette for *Sports Car Illustrated* magazine in 1956 (*Sports Car Illustrated* changed its title to *Car and Driver* in 1961). In his opening paragraph, Ludvigsen stated that the Corvette was "... as much a dual-purpose machine as a stock Jaguar, Triumph or Austin Healey" and that GM was now building a real sports car. Ludvigsen still had reservations, however. He didn't like the non-adjustable steering wheel position, nor the upright seat backs. As for the handling, Ludvigsen considered the steering a bit on the spongy side and wasn't happy with the strong understeer, but added that quite a few foreign sports cars suffered from the same faults. During the forties and fifties American car makers seemed to forget that, as well as giving their machines plenty of go, they had to make them stop as well. The Corvette was no exception, Ludvigsen reporting that the brakes "... faded almost into oblivion during the performance tests." Overall, Ludvigsen summed up the Corvette as being an excellent car, and other motoring scribes thought likewise.

Although it still had a long way to go, the Corvette had the potential to become a great sports car in the best European tradition. As if to prove the point, Arkus-Duntov took a Corvette to Daytona in January 1956. It had the Duntov cam, of course, producing 240 hp, while the addition of high-compression heads added a further 10 horses. Duntov was pretty sure one of his prepared Corvettes would make the flying mile at 150 mph. Although the conditions at the beach weren't exactly the best, the Corvette managed a two-way run at 150.583 mph. Thereafter Corvettes were entered in several competitions coast to

Previous pages: last of a ten-year design, the 1962 Corvette looks tastefully elegant as it reposes in the beautiful Cypress Gardens not far from Orlando, Florida. Top: crossed flags are the trademark of one of the world's great cars. Right: rear view of the Sting Ray shows off the sleekness and unity of design to advantage.

coast and even in some European events. At Daytona Speed Weeks Corvette had a head-to-head with a race-prepared Thunderbird. The T-Bird won the production standing mile, but in the modified class, Corvette won handsomely.

While the Corvette did well, it failed to win – until the 1956 Pebble Beach races. The way things were on that day, Corvette's chances looked very slim. Dr. Dick Thompson was experienced with Porsche racing but knew little about Corvettes, yet he had to drive one in the race because the great Walt Hangsen had fallen ill at the last minute. As if to show how little he knew about 'Vettes, at the start of the race he flooded the outsize carburetors, and by the time the car started, several others had dashed by. Imagine the excitement when Dr. Dick Thompson drove the Corvette into the lead. The crowd was on its feet cheering Dr. Dick, who looked as mild-mannered as Clark Kent but was as tough as King Kong as he fought to retain the lead. Then the one thing we mentioned earlier let the Corvette – and the good doctor – down. The car's drum brakes faded into the back of beyond, never to return. A Mercedes gullwing pipped the Corvette to the post, but the car still managed second place, plus first in class. Not yet a winner, perhaps, but at least Corvette had joined the club!

GM's faith in its sports car began to pay off. By the end of the 1956 sales year, 3,467 Corvettes had been built. Compared to the miserable 1955 total, this was a great and encouraging leap forward. The accountants were nonplussed!

Renewed with vigor, Corvette drove into 1957 little changed externally. Zora Arkus-Duntov is first and foremost a European. He grew up with European cars and trained in Germany, the mecca of European technology. It goes without saying, therefore, that his ideas were probably more advanced than those of his paymasters in Detroit. American car makers' philosophy was – and still is to some extent – maximum profit. Make it flash, but skimp on real quality; in Europe and even in Japan, the opposite is true. Many are the clever American engineers whose good ideas are rejected by accountants as being too costly. Fortunately, Duntov's persistence overcame many of the frustrations placed in his way, and he did not hesitate to state his views. Perhaps this was how Corvette and Chevrolet became the first American cars to feature fuel injection in 1957.

GM's engineering division had been experimenting with fuel injection for some time in the hope there might be some viable way it could be applied to cars. Up to the point at which Duntov stepped in, the program had been run by John Dolza, who was the system's principal engineer. Others involved were E.A. Kehoe and Donald Stoltman. Also much involved was Ed Cole, who was determined that Chevrolet should have fuel injection in 1957, no matter what difficulties had to be surmounted. There was much humming and hawing, let's-wait-and-see-how-long-we-can-drag-our-feet-on-this-one, from the accountants when suddenly Plymouth and Ford seized the initiative. They had all-new, very exciting models for 1957, making Chevrolet's moderate face-lift of the 1955 body a non-starter by comparison. Funny how thinking changes with time. Today

Previous pages and right: a fine example of a 1962 Corvette, this one fitted with the removable hardtop roof. Removal of the roof requires two people at best. Strips atop the fenders are survivors of the chrome-laden 1958 model, while a more restrained grille replaced the car's earlier toothy grin.

a 1957 Chevrolet fetches three times what the other two do on the collector circuit. Attitudes changed in a hurry; the threat of Ford and Plymouth was too great to pass by, and at the last minute fuel injection was given the go-ahead.

Although Ed Cole got his wish, Duntov, Dolza and the rest of the team were still working to perfect the system. As *Sports Cars Illustrated* noticed, Chevrolet's fuel injection was a "premature baby," but one that was "alive and kicking." Premature or not, the Rochester-built system, christened Ramjet, worked well enough for several hundred people to order this $675 option.

Ramjet worked on the principle that each cylinder had its own injector feeding a continuous flow of fuel under controlled conditions. The fuel is atomized into a pressurized spray and fed directly into the intake ports. The amount of fuel delivered depends on the air flow, which is controlled by accelerator pedal pressure. It enters a chamber which splits into separate nozzles called ram tubes that lead to each cylinder. On the way the air meets the fuel that is continuously being sprayed and is blended into a precisely controlled amount of air/fuel mixture which is fed into each cylinder.

There were problems, though. The injectors would clog and were susceptible to dirt and poor fuel. Rough idling was another trouble spot caused by too much heat absorption by the injectors. These faults were eventually ironed out in what one might call a program of continuous development. But there was a bonus not actually planned by the engineers.

For 1957 the engine's displacement was raised to 283 cubic inches. This engine, equipped with dual quad carburetors, developed 270 hp; with fuel injection the

1963 SPECIFICATIONS

Engine: Ohv V-8, water-cooled cast-iron block and head. Bore and stroke: 4.00 x 3.25ins. Bhp: 360 @ 6000. Compression ratio: 11.25:1. Carburetion: Ramjet fuel injection.

Chassis: Front suspension: Independent; upper and lower A- arms, coil springs, tubular hydraulic shock absorbers, anti-roll bar. Rear suspension: Independent; fixed differential, U-jointed halfshafts, lateral struts, radius rods, transverse leaf spring, tubular hydraulic shock absorbers. Steering: Saginaw recirculating- ball; 17:1 overall ratio; 3.4 turns lock-to-lcck. Brakes: Self- adjusting 11-in. dia.; 4-wheel cast-iron drums with hydraulic acutation; 135 sq. in. effective lining area; sintered-metallic linings optional. Transmission: Close-ratio 4-speed manual with floor shift. Final drive ratio: 3.70:1.

Measurements: Weight: 315.0lbs. Tire size: 6.70 x 15 4- ply. Track: 56.3 front, 57.0 rear. Wheelbase: 98.0" Overall length: 175.3" Overall width: 69.6" Overall height: 49.8" Maximum speed: 118mph. Fuel consumption: N/A.

These and previous pages: the 1963 Corvette Sting Ray was as close to perfect as any sports car had a right to be. Responsibility for the timeless design belonged to Bill Mitchell and Bob McLean, while the mechanics were the work of Zora Arkus-Duntov. Surprising how so many Europeans wax lyrical about the Jaguar E-Type – and quite rightfully so – yet ignore the Sting Ray, which is every bit its equal.

horsepower was 283. In other words, one hp per cu. in. This was quite an accomplishment, and one that Chevrolet quickly took advantage of in its advertising and promotions blurb. After all, its not everybody who can boast one horsepower per cubic inch.

DeSoto had one hp. per cu. in. in 1957 but forgot to mention the fact to the world.

Using its 345-cubic-inch hemi equipped with dual 4 bbl carburetors, DeSoto managed 345 horsepower in its wild and woolly Adventurer model. Motoring types picked up the implications but DeSoto didn't. Chrysler Corp., always at the forefront when it came to engineering, was having a field day in 1957 with its beautifully styled cars. Perhaps DeSoto thought the extra publicity wasn't needed. In 1961, as the last DeSoto rolled off the line, its soon-to-be-out-of-work executives probably wished they had publicized one horsepower per cubic inch when they had the chance. Had they done so, perhaps DeSoto might have survived a little longer.

Chevrolet, as we know, didn't make that mistake and it made sure all the motoring media knew about fuel injection and 283/283 as well. *Sports Cars Illustrated* compared a dual quad with 270 hp and the 283/283 fuelie. There was hardly any difference in performance; the FI ran to 60 mph in 6.6 seconds, the dual quad in 6.8 seconds. Where they did find a difference was in response. The carbureted car was slower to respond to a heavy right foot, whilst the FI's answer was instantaneous. The irrepressible and great motoring scribe, Tom McCahill, managed 0-60 in 6.2 seconds and claimed a top speed close to 140 mph. Uncle Tom, as he was fondly known, was a tall man, so his major gripe was about the room, or lack of it, in the driver's seat. Unlike the main competitor, the Thunderbird, Corvette

did not have an adjustable steering column. "… the steering column cannot be moved in or out to fit the driver," wrote McCahill. "Tie this up with shallow, small seats and you have a car that is suitable for men on the smallish side only … the cockpit is now much too small for football players." Overall, however, the tester, who caused more white hair in the halls of Detroit than anyone else, thought the Corvette "… a great American high performance car, the greatest ever made." No doubt the sighs of relief heard at Chevrolet's head offices were loud and long!

Out of a total of 6,339 Corvettes built for 1957 1,040 were fuel injected. Total production brought a song to the hearts of all those committed to the Corvette's success. Almost double the 1956 figure, the additional sales were put down to aggressive advertising of the car's sporting successes, fuel injection, and the rumors circulating that

Facing page top: base engine was the 327-cubic-inch unit rated at 250 bhp; the version illustrated was the next in line with 300 bhp on tap in carbureted form. A wide-ratio manual four-speed Borg-Warner transmission was available, while a close-ratio version was offered with the bigger engines. Facing page bottom: neatly designed taillights reflect Sting Ray's powerful personality. Top: dashboard layout is attractive, with legible instruments grouped in line of vision. Fake bits and pieces still persisted as the simulated knock-off hubs bear out. Right: the crossed flags motif was an excellent design by some unnamed hero in GM's styling studios and a fitting symbol for a great car.

the two place T-Bird would be no more after 1957: it was to become a four-seat hardtop instead. This was welcome news to Chevrolet; now the Corvette was very definitely number one in a field of one.

Although everybody immediately thinks of the fuel-injected 283/283, Corvette had other engines as well. All displaced 283 cubic inches, but developed different horsepower; the smallest engine was rated at 245 hp with two four-bbl carbs. This was followed by the 270 hp version, again with twin four barrels. The standard engine developed 220 hp with a single four barrel. Three "fuelies" were on tap: the 250 horse and two 283s. One of these was the high-performance engine which sported a tachometer on the steering column. Options included a new four-speed manual transmission at $175, heavy-duty racing suspension costing $725, and three Positraction rear axles with ratios from 3.70:1 to 4.56:1. All cost $45 each.

One anomaly about Corvette; it never followed a trend. In 1955 when car sales were so huge they threatened to sink America beneath a sea of metal, Corvette production was way down on 1954. Then, in 1958, the year of Eisenhower's "mini recession," car sales sagged dismally. Not Corvette, though. Production rose to an unprecedented – for Corvette – 9,168 units.

Before heading into 1958, it might be worth mentioning Corvette's competition challenge, the beautiful Corvette SS. Ed Cole and Duntov decided, after the promising show Corvettes made in 1956, to really go to town for 1957. Various European racing cars such as the Jaguar D-Type were studied, and Harley Earl suggested shoe horning a Chevy V-8 under the hood of a D-Type, restyling the body and racing it at Sebring. Fortunately that idea was nipped in the bud by Duntov, who drew up his own plans on how the racing Corvette should look.

By the time the car, code-named XP-64, was ready it weighed 100 lbs. less than the Jaguar D-Type. Under the magnesium body was a tubular frame, a de Dion rear axle (Duntov would have preferred independent suspension) and, surprisingly, Chrysler "Center-Plane" front drum brakes which were adapted for all four wheels! Chevrolet didn't have decent enough binders at the time, it seems, and although Delco was experimenting with discs, they wouldn't be ready in time.

As already noted, the wind-tunnel-tested SS was a magnificent looking car. Under the hood was an enlarged 283 fuel-injected V-8 developing 310 horsepower. A four-speed manual transmission was the only choice for gearing and the SS had a Positraction differential thrown in for good measure. Its dry weight was only 1,850 lbs. for a length of 168 inches. As for the body shape, it had the familiar toothy Corvette grille, and a sculptured hood with three sets of air vents for cooling. The whole front end lifted forward to expose the engine, front suspension, wheels and brakes, pre-dating modern Corvettes by 27 years! Behind the driver's head was arranged a bullet-shaped pod that acted as a stylish headrest.

Amid much publicity the SS made its début at the 1957 Sebring 12-hour race. Chevrolet had hoped to sign up the world's greatest drivers – Juan Fangio and Stirling Moss both drove the car, liked it, but expressed reservations and stayed with Maserati. Instead, Chevrolet picked John Fitch,

Previous pages and right: although almost identical to the 1963 model, changes are apparent on this 1965 example. The much debated split rear backlight became one piece in 1964; rear pillar vents were made functional, and rocker panel trim was altered. Seen from a low angle (right) the Sting Ray looks particularly mean.

who also happened to be team manager. His back-up was Piero Taruffi, who had to fly 6,000 miles to be at the race on time.

Sebring 1957. Assembled in readiness for the great 12-hour endurance race was the might of Europe. Ferrari, Maserati, Jaguar, plus one solitary Corvette SS, a car that had never raced before and wasn't really ready to race that day. A David among a bunch of Goliaths. Unlike in the bible story, the Goliaths won. The SS was fast and very competitive, but its brakes weren't. Then there were engine problems and finally the suspension appeared to give up. That was it, and the SS retired after the twenty-third lap. Not an auspicious day for Chevrolet.

What caused the car to retire was simplicity itself. A small rubber bushing inadvertently split during assembly. It was located at the chassis end of one of the lower rods that supplied the de Dion tube with lateral support. The whole car crippled because of wrong assembly of the rubber bushing!

Down but not out, Chevrolet prepared to ready a team of three SS Corvettes for Le Mans. Hardly had Corvette staggered to its feet, when it was laid out for the count by an order from on high: no more competition, no more racing. This was immediately followed by the American Manufacturers' Association ban on any U.S. car company racing or advertising in a way that might suggest racing or performance. GM told Chevrolet to kill off the SS program and that was that.

This Sting Ray is a beautiful example of the breed, with a perfect interior to match. B-pillar vents on the right hand side of the car are fake, while the ones on the driver's side are functional. Boat-tail design was a Sting Ray trademark and is complemented by the fuel filler cap. The engine in this car is the 396 rated at 425 bhp.

Without a racing program any more, Chevrolet would have to do the best it could with the Corvette. At this point we return to 1958, when Corvette scored its highest ever sales in a year when for everyone else the opposite was true. Perhaps one of the reasons why the 1958 model did so well was its change of direction. Now that Chevrolet was unable to race it, the Corvette became more of a powerful boulevard cruiser, attracting those who didn't care for the race-track, dirt-in-the-face image. Moreover, they preferred to be noticed in their own small town or cruising through Beverly Hills hoping some movie producer might notice. Then there were the professional classes who thought life was more than the back seat of a Cadillac.

Not everybody was enamored with the 1958 facelift, for along the way the Corvette had gained weight. Overall length jumped by 9 inches to 177, width from 71 inches to 73, yet the wheelbase remained at 102 inches. In addition, various styling nuances gave the car the appearance of more girth than it actually had: such as the larger grille teeth, and although there were only nine instead of thirteen, in 1958 they protruded more. Then there were two egg-shaped hollows either side of the grille. Matt black paint gave this impression, for no hollows existed – yet if extra cooling for the brakes was required, real hollows could easily be provided.

Other external changes included dual headlights, a louvered hood and chrome "straps" on the trunk lid – rather similar to the chrome pieces on Pontiac hoods of a few years earlier. And the twin front bumpers extended through the hollows to attach to the frame, thus adding considerable strength.

A 160 mph speedometer might have been wishful thinking, but it was a great improvement on earlier Corvettes. White on black in a hooded crescent shape was clear and concise. Ahead of the speedometer, directly in front of the driver was the tach in a round dial. Other instruments were set in smaller dials, flanking the tachometer. A center console and seat belts were standard, but few people cared for the bucket seats, complaining that one sat on them, not in them.

Under the hood the standard engine developed 230 hp. The other two engines with two four-bbl carburetors were rated at 245 and 270 hp. Of the two fuel injection offerings, one was 250, the other 290 hp. A base 1958 Corvette convertible cost $3,591; once all the desirable and necessary options (heavy-duty suspension and brakes at $780) had been added, the buyer was looking at $1,500 extra.

Hood louvers and the chrome trunk "straps" were deleted on the otherwise unchanged 1959 Corvette. Minor improvements, such as concave gauge lenses and relocated armrests, consolidated an already good interior design. Even the seats were improved for 1959. Like all American cars of the time, the Corvette's option list was long; three transmissions (two, three and four speeds, the two speed being Powerglide), four final drive ratios, three brake choices and two suspensions. Five variations of the 283 V-8 were offered, but were unchanged from 1958. Sales went up again, this time to 9,670 units and the base price rose to $3,875. Although sales had yet to reach the magic 10,000 mark, after six years on the market, Corvette had become very much a part of the American way of life and there was no sign it would ever be dropped.

Compared to almost all other American cars offered in 1959, Corvette would have won the conservative styling award hands down. Teardrop taillights, canted fins, star-

scraper fins, wrap over, wrap round windshields, chrome heading every which way – that was the surrealistic manner in which Detroit ended the great fifties decade. Whatever anyone says, the cars of the fifties were truly expressions of art on wheels and very little else. For that they are memorable, a wonderful selection of New World culture never to be repeated.

A new decade began and three compacts, the conventional Ford Falcon, the pretty Plymouth Valiant and the revolutionary Chevrolet Corvair, took their bow. As American Motors found out with its Rambler, people were tiring of excess; they wanted a return to basics. Hence the rush to build compacts. The rest of the industry toned down some of their wildest 1959 designs, but Corvette sauntered into 1960 little changed.

10,261! Corvette finally cracked the 10,000 barrier and sales never again went below that figure. Changes to the two fuel-injected engines were the only difference; one needed a keen eye and hearing sharply attuned to engine notes to discern between 1959 and 1960. Power was increased to 275 and 315 horsepower, the latter equipped with solid lifters and boasting a 11.0:1 compression ratio. The 275 retained the hydraulic lifters. Aluminum clutch housings saved eighteen pounds, and cars with the Duntov cam had aluminum radiators. At the beginning of the 1960 model run, Chevrolet offered cast aluminum heads as an option. As is common with aluminum heads however, there were problems due to their proneness to warp when overheated, necessitating their replacement. To make matters worse, quality control was not what it should have been and the heads were withdrawn.

No doubt about it, the 1960 Corvette, even though a sun, sand and surf car, could really perform well with the 315 hp engine. According to *Sports Car Illustrated* 0-60 took a mere 6.7 seconds, just a tenth of a second slower than a 250 GT Ferrari. When it came to top speed the Ferrari would be hale and hearty and roaring on when the Corvette was staggering around out of breath, nevertheless, the small block 283 was an extremely good engine and not one that would be as temperamental as a Ferrari, more often in the workshop than on the road.

Bill Mitchell had replaced the retiring Harley Earl as chief designer in the late fifties and the first sign of his influence appeared on the 1961 Corvette. The rear deck was flatter and sharper in profile than before, and the taillights were moved from above the fenders to a new location each side of the license plate holder and now comprised twin recessed round lights on either side. From a design point of view the 1961 and 1962 Corvette was an interesting car inasmuch as Harley Earl was responsible for the front, Mitchell the rear. For the first time in its youthful life, Corvette lost its teeth. These were replaced by a horizontal mesh. In place of the Corvette circular medallion was a crossed flags motif with Corvette spelled out in block letters below it.

The bulging hood on this 1967 Sting Ray (previous pages and above) tells us that the largest of the available engines lurks beneath. This was the awesome 427-cubic-inch V8 rated at 390 bhp in this car. If that was still not enough, buyers could have 400 or 435 bhp and, if the speedometer is anything to go by, a top speed of 160 mph.

1967 CORVETTE STING RAY COUPE 327/300HP

An interesting point worthy of mention is Bill Mitchell's interest in the Corvette. A true car buff, Mitchell had money and was able to afford to dabble a bit in his favorite sport: motor racing. His idea was to field a racing team of his own and he picked Corvette to be the car.

When work had been proceeding on the ill-fated SS, a test vehicle was created for research and development. Clad in a rough fiberglass body the car, nicknamed the "Mule," did all the dirty work. After Sebring the Mule was taken away to have a similar body to the SS installed in readiness for the Le Mans that never came. With GM out of racing, Bill Mitchell said he would like to have the ex-Mule. His bosses agreed, but only on condition that if the car was raced it would have a new body and be a private entrant financed with outside money.

The Sting Ray, as Mitchell's Corvette was prophetically named, was designed within GM's styling department and was very low, used the SS frame, and was fabricated from fiberglass reinforced with aluminum. One look at the shape and the 1963 Corvette is immediately apparent. On the mechanical side, the Sting Ray used a stock 283 engine rated at 300 bhp.

Zora Arkus-Duntov lent a hand, Larry Shinoda, one of the top stylists, put his finishing touches to the design, and Dr. Dick Thompson turned up again to drive. In its first SCCA race in 1959 poor brakes let the Sting Ray down but it managed fourth place on its inaugural outing. In 1960 with better brakes the Sting Ray came second in a toughly contested race featuring all the top European racers. Marvelously, the Sting Ray was just beaten by a cool, race-bred Maserati. Considering the sponsorship and big money professional racing attracts, Bill Mitchell's shoestring budget operation was commendable, to say the least.

Corvette's production total went to 10,939 in 1961; no doubt this was helped by a Chevrolet-sponsored TV drama entitled *Route 66*. The show had premiered in the autumn of 1960 and was an immediate hit, telling of the adventures of two young men (Martin Milner and George Maharis) who drive round America on the old Route 66 in a 1960 Corvette. They must have been very wealthy young men; they had the very latest Corvette at the start of each new season. Unquestionably the various Corvettes became the stars of each season's series and are probably the most memorable part of what were otherwise very simple and predictable scripts. Remember the Mustang and the Charger in *Bullitt*? – everyone does. It was the greatest chase scene ever filmed and to this day folk will remember that, but little else in what was a very competent movie.

For 1962 Corvette had some big news nestling under the hood. More power – much more! Chevy's engineers bored and stroked the 283 to 327 cubic inches. The standard engine was rated at 250 horsepower. Three options were offered: 300, 340 and 360. Only the 360 hp engine was fuel injected. All engines bar the 250 hp offering were given a longer duration cam, heavier duty bearing and larger ports. As before, the Duntov cam and solid lifters were specified for the top engine.

Bodily, there was little to distinguish the car from 1961, yet it gave more of an impression of being a thoroughbred, as the designers removed the chrome outline round the recessed "coves" along the front of the sides, eliminating the contrasting color scheme. A smarter looking simulated air vent replaced the traditional three spears.

Car and Driver road-tested a 1962 Corvette in. its December 1961 issue. For the test the 360 hp fuelie was picked and the testers got a 0-60 run of 6.9 seconds with

the four-speed manual, and 8.8 with the horrible two-speed Powerglide. Whichever way you look at it, this was impressive. The times with the 360 might have been bettered had the car had Positraction. It didn't, and the testers experienced rear wheel hop, a feature that plagued Corvette during its life with a solid rear axle. Though not without criticism. *Car and Driver* summed up by saying the Corvette was one of the most exciting cars to drive and relatively inexpensive at that.

The year 1962 was a great one for Corvette; 14,531 units were built. Base price was now $4,038 for a convertible but, with all the desirable knick-knacks thrown in, the car hovered around six grand. For what the buyer got, $6,000 was still a good price compared to some of the highly strung European sports cars.

This was also to be the last year for this particular Corvette style. In its nine years it had become a well-established, well-respected automobile of the kind Europeans thought America could never produce. As each year went by, so the Corvette improved. But the best was yet to come. Being readied in the wings for autumn introduction was a staggering new Corvette. It had been rumored for the previous couple of years, but now the time was at hand for the Sting Ray to become public. In a year when John Glenn became the first American in space, when Marilyn Monroe supposedly committed suicide, and a little-known Merseyside group called the Beatles topped a local Liverpool poll, the Corvette Sting Ray would cap the sensational new stories.

Nineteen sixty-seven was the last year for the Sting Ray, one of the great sports cars of all time. Production for the year was 22,940, some 5,000 down on 1966.

CHAPTER THREE
THE WINNAH IS …

"Compared with previous Corvettes, the Sting Ray is improved in almost every imaginable respect … " So wrote the excellent *Car and Driver* magazine on its test report of the 1963 Corvette Sting Ray. This was conservative praise; the new Corvette was an American automotive revolution. Nothing like it had come out of Detroit before; as Mr. Duntov said in a *Car and Driver* interview, it was a car that he would be "proud to drive in Europe."

The design for this radical new car had started with Bill Mitchell's racing Sting Ray and a special styling exercise based on the rear-engined Corvair, the Q-Corvette. Mitchell wanted to see a brand new Corvette, his own Corvette, and by 1959 he and his design team had taken styling cues from the aforementioned vehicles, putting them together in an experimental project called XP-720. This became the beginning of the 1963 Sting Ray – the embryo, as it were.

Various ideas, some radical, some not quite so, had been considered during the gestation of the Sting Ray. Solid, conservative GM, of all companies, had become tolerant of new approaches to automobile design – the rear-engined Corvair compact was a good case in point – and it was easier for Cole, Duntov, Mitchell and others to give vent to fresh concepts in automobile design. Some ideas, such as mid-engined layouts, were shelved, but Duntov was adamant that the new Corvette should have independent rear suspension, causing much uncertainty in the minds of the decision makers until Duntov whispered that IRS would probably sell 30,000 Corvettes a year. To the

management that was persuasive – the Sting Ray got independent suspension….

There was much more to the Sting Ray than independent rear suspension. A new ladder-type chassis with five crossmembers replaced the old X-frame. The ladder configuration would be able to handle larger engines and provide the strength to handle the increased lateral stresses Duntov's design would bring.

Duntov's new chassis was shorter by four inches – 98 against 102 – than the old X-frame, and to obtain better weight distribution, driver and passenger were placed further to the rear. This allowed the engine and transmission to be moved back to what is called a "front mid-engine" location. Weight distribution with the 327-cubic-inch, 340 hp engine and the 20 gallon gas tank full, worked out at almost 50/50.

As for the independent rear suspension, Duntov based it upon his CERV 1 (Chevrolet Experimental Research Vehicle), which was a single-seater racing car design similar to the Formula 1 cars of the day. A differential was mounted in the frame on rubber-cushioned struts, which reduced ride harshness. The U-jointed half-shafts were tied together by what many considered an antiquated development – a transverse leaf spring which attached to the rear of the differential case. Control arms were positioned each side of the casing in a lateral and slightly forward location and extended to a hub carrier with a large radius rod behind it. All relatively ingenious but simple in operation. The half-shafts functioned like upper control arms, the lower ones took care of vertical wheel motion and trailing rods looked after fore and aft wheel motion. Finally, the shock absorbers were conventional twin-tube units. Front suspension consisted of unequal upper and lower A-arms, concentric

coil springs, shocks and an anti-roll bar. Recirculating ball steering geared at 19.6:1 was quicker than before.

Base engine was the 250 horsepower 327, and the three optional units were the same as 1962. Unusual for such an advanced car – remember the Ferrari 250GT still had a live rear axle – was the provision of drum brakes. Sintered metallic brakes were a $37.70 option, but where

Facing page top: the interior of the 1967 model was little different from that of 1963, but mild evolutionary changes to the body were improvements that resulted in a very clean, cohesive shape.

were the discs? Another two years would pass before these would become available. As before, the base transmission was a close ratio three-speed manual box with a meaty four-speed manual and anaemic two-speed Powerglide automatic, the latter for the boulevard cruisers, as reasonably priced options.

Today the Bill Mitchell 1963 Corvette Sting Ray styling is regarded as the most desirable of all on the collectors' market. This is hardly surprising, for the Sting Ray was a work of art, from its pointed front end with its revolving hidden quad lights, the spear-shaped bulge on the hood, the creaseline across the roof and ending in the boat-tail rear deck. Ease of entry and exit was facilitated by the coupé's doors, which were cut into the roof. Twin dummy hood vents, one either side of the "spear" and on the coupé's rear pillars, were frowned upon by the motoring press as unnecessary kitsch. But the one outstanding item that makes a 1963 Corvette so much more collectable than any other is the split rear window.

No one but Mitchell wanted the split rear window, most being of the opinion that it would be a hazard to the rear view; neither Duntov nor the motoring journals liked it. Mitchell apparently said that if the partition wasn't allowed to stay then "… you might as well forget the whole thing". Meaning, I suppose, the complete body shape. As we now know, Bill Mitchell had the last word and got his way. But only for 1963; in 1964 the partition was replaced by a single window.

The interior was functional and well laid out. Twin semicircular hoods formed the dash, in the center the "control tower" leading into the console smacked of earlier 'Vettes. All instruments were mounted directly in front of the driver and shielded by one of the hoods. Two large dials flanked by a pair of smaller ones either side were very legible through the deeply dished, three-spoke steering wheel. A clock and radio took up the "control tower" space.

After the criticism meted out by testers over the years, the car's interior had obviously been given a lot of thought. The seats were better designed for comfort and adjustment; *Car and Driver* reported that their drivers, who ranged between 5ft. 7in. and 6ft. 4in., were able to find almost ideal seating positions. The steering also came in for some improvement, for not only was it now light and positive without power assist, but it had a three-inch adjustment as well. This car must have made Uncle Tom McCahill very happy. He may not have been pleased with the luggage space, though, for while there was plenty of room behind the rear seats to stow the month's groceries, it was getting them there that was the problem. Due to cost considerations, neither the coupé nor the convertible were given a trunk lid of any description. Imagine on a rainy night trying to place the groceries through the doors, then getting them behind the seats. As for the convertible, the folded top had to be removed first!

From zero to 60 in 6.2 seconds with the 350 bhp engine and four-speed box certainly put the Corvette in the big

Faster than a freight train? Probably. The train behind this 1967 427-cubic-inch, 390 bhp Sting Ray (previous pages) may be nothing but a blur, but the chances are that the sleek roadster would beat it in a side-by-side dash. As can be seen from this front view (right), the Sting Ray was a magnificent design and easily the equal of the best that Europe could offer.

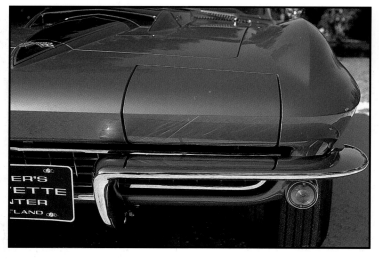

Facing page top: the back end of the convertible was a carry-over from the 1961 'Vette which took this design cue from the soon-to-be-introduced 1963 Sting Ray. Facing page left: now you see them, now you don't. Disappearing headlights have remained with Corvette to this day. Facing page right: GM was justly proud to have its Mark of Excellence sticker affixed to a Sting Ray. Note the massive width of the doors! Top: interior is smart and functional, with steering wheel finished in fake wood, and the seats are comfortable. Above: "427" badge hints at the power tethered under the hood.

league. Top speed with the fuel injected 327/360 was in the order of 140 mph, possibly faster. Along with Mitchell's beautiful 1963 Buick Riviera, to which it bore absolutely no resemblance, the Corvette Sting Ray was one of the finest looking cars ever to take to the road, and the public loved it. As a styling exercise it has few peers; possibly the '55/57 T-Birds, the Gullwing Mercedes, Jaguar E-type and one or two Ferraris equal the Sting Ray; 21,513 Sting Rays were built during the 1963 model year, and of these, 10,594 were coupés, and 10,919 convertibles.

Of the little-changed 1964 Sting Ray 22,229 units were built; 8,304 coupés, the rest convertibles, suggesting that people preferred the convertible over the fastback by quite a high margin. Sales were almost equal in 1963, yet in 1964 the difference was over 5,000. Little was changed from 1963 except the rear window, which lost the controversial partition. Perhaps the buyer favored the partition, hence the drastic drop in coupé sales.

Chevrolet engineering had done an excellent job of eliminating the Corvette's well known squeaks and rattles caused by the fiberglass panels flexing and moving whilst the car was in motion – a problem that had existed from conception until 1962. Almost twice as much steel support was used for the '63 model, without any appreciable gain in weight. This was accomplished by reducing the fiberglass thickness and applied to the 1965 to 1967 models as well. Applying the extra steel reinforcements cut out virtually all the creaks and groans liable to drive those with sensitive hearing to the point of distraction.

The 1964 changes were minimal – why interfere with a good thing? – and while the single rear window improved visibility it didn't look as good. Bill Mitchell was right; the partition added greatly to the overall design. Apart from

American automobiles have always been big on options and Corvette was no exception. Compare this 1967 model (these, previous pages and overleaf) with other examples illustrated in this book – each is different. This one has side exhausts, different wheels, and the biggest engine option – 435 bhp with triple two barrels! This engine had solid lifters, transistorized electronic ignition, and an 11:1 compression ratio.

the dummy hood vents which went the way of all silly ideas, the Sting Ray was untouched. On the instruments, brushed aluminum at the center of the dials was removed in favor of all-black surfaces.

Horsepower was increased for two of the four engines, the 340 jumping to 365 and the old fuelie 360 was now 375. A long list of options could push the $4,037 price for the convertible to $6,000 with ease. Take genuine aluminum knock-off wheels for example. They were twenty cents under $323 and the special sintered brake lining package was $629.

The next three years saw a number of improvements to what was becoming recognized the world over as a sports car with class. Even the British auto magazines, whose arrogance when it comes to American machinery has to be read to be believed, actually praised the Sting Ray. *Motor* said it was the fastest car it had ever tested and the four-speed gearbox one of the "...best we have ever encountered."

The big news for 1965 were the brakes. At long last America's only sports car was to have brakes that fitted its otherwise robust image. Drums were out; discs were in – on all four wheels. Although others were beginning to offer front discs as an option, only Corvette had four-wheel discs as standard. This was a wise move in light of the powerhouse engine the Sting Ray was tempting buyers with. Displacing 396 cubic inches, this savage unit developed a mean 425 horses, could reach 60 in 5.6 seconds and cover the standing quarter mile in 14 seconds at a speed of 104 mph. That is fast for an off-the-showroom-floor automobile that sold for under $5,000. What European could have possibly delivered that kind of shattering performance with handling and brakes to match for that sort of money? The answer is, quite simply, none.

Another version of the 327-cubic-inch engine was also made available for those who wanted plenty of performance without having to go hog-wild. This was the 350-hp unit which delivered its performance in a smoother, more refined package. For those who still wanted it, the fuel injected 375 horsepower engine was in its final year.

If anybody mourned the passing of the fuelie, 1966 saw a terrifying engine take its place. This was the 427 cubic inch bomb that could be specified with either 390 or 425 horsepower. Both replaced the 396 cid engine of the previous year and if you thought the 396/425 was good then, as the great Rolling Stones might have said, you got "...no satisfaction" until you tried 427/425. This one just blew you away – puff! Like Peter, Paul and Mary's Magic Dragon, you were gone. How does 0-60 in 4.8 seconds and 12.8 seconds to reach 112 mph in the standing quarter grab you? Those were the days, my friends, those were the days....

Apart from Chrysler's vicious hemis nothing could touch Chevrolet's 427. Except perhaps Ford's 427. Carroll Shelby used this engine in his immortal Cobras, and those Cobras were dangerous indeed. Ford and Chrysler believed in competition in the Swinging Sixties, but GM's top brass said no to Chevrolet trying to participate – it was not the General's practice to go racing. Even though Chevy didn't race, it couldn't build enough Corvettes to keep up with the demand. In 1965 23,562 had been built; in 1966 27,720. The St. Louis plant was working extra shifts and still couldn't make enough cars to meet demand.

Big block Sting Rays are easy to identify; they have a special hood with a protuberant bulge down the center that looks not unlike a rocket ship, the bulge swelling out as it gets closer to the windshield. On normal hoods – now flat and without the indentations used to highlight the

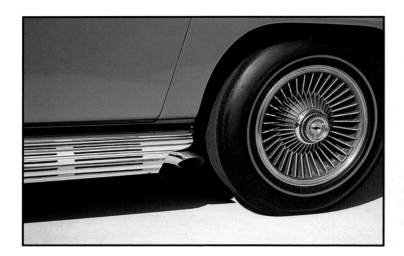

Top: redline tires were all the rage in the late Sixties. With no trunk lid there was little choice but to store the spare beneath the car.

fake air vents – the spear-shaped bulge continued. Three slots on each side of the front fenders were functional.

After the relative calm and compassion of the fifties, the sixties were troubled times, and in 1967 the problems multiplied; not for Corvette, though. This was the Sting Ray's last year. It really should have been 1966 that the last Sting Ray was built, but its successor wasn't ready and Duntov asked that the car be put back a year until various wind-tunnel tests had been satisfactorily completed.

Five slots on the fenders replaced the previous year's three, but overall the 1967 Sting Ray was little changed. The knock-off wheel option was deleted due to safety regulations, which were beginning to bite. The standard engine was of 327 cubic inches and 300 horsepower, but there were four 427 units to choose from. Smallest was 390 horses, followed by 400, 430 and 435. One other 327 rated at 350 hp was also available. The basic price of a Sting Ray convertible had crept to $4,240.75. As *Mad's* Alfred E. Neuman used to say: "Cheap at the price!"

Nineteen sixty-seven was the Sting Ray's last year, but the car's design, like the Ferrari GTO's, has endured over the years. Succeeding Corvettes may have been – and are – better cars, but none will ever match Bill Mitchell's near-perfect lines. There was no mistaking a Sting Ray for anything else other than the true sports car it was – a Michigan Yankee in Modena's court if you like. Detroit had accomplished the one thing nobody thought it would ever do: it beat the Europeans at their own game.

CHAPTER FOUR
1968-1982 – AN OASIS IN THE WILDERNESS

Bill Mitchell had a liking for sharks. He loved to watch their movements in the water and thought their shape graceful and perfectly suited to their environment. It was this marauder of the deep that led to Mitchell's Mako Shark show car, and was closely followed by the Mako Shark II that traveled the auto show circuits in 1965. This non-functional car was used to gauge public reaction to the design which would eventually end up as the 1968 Corvette.

On the car front in 1968 all hell seemed to break loose. Muscle cars suddenly became the order of the day, with huge seven-liter engines powering Mustangs, Plymouth Road Runners and Chevelles in wavy lines down the road. Some, such as Dodge/Plymouth, aimed their advertising directly at the drug culture element, with psychedelic illustrations and hippie-style prose. Obviously it worked because Dodge/Plymouth sold a lot of cars during 1968/69. As for the new Corvette, number one in a field of one (with apologies to Alfred E. Neuman), it was able to remain above the muscle car business.

It was a radically different Corvette that emerged for 1968. Its lines were taken directly from the Mako Shark II show car which Bill Mitchell's team had created. Although others, like the famous designer Larry Shinoda, had a major part in the development of the Mako Shark II, it was Mitchell who laid the groundwork and said what he should like to see. What he, Duntov, and Chevrolet engineering would

like to have seen and what they actually got were two entirely different things.

There had always been talk of mid-rear-engined formats, and the teams involved with developing the 1968 Corvette assumed this would be the way it would go. Chevrolet Engineering Center, under Frank Winchell, thought up a compact design powered by a 327-cubic-inch engine, but too much weight bias at the rear made this idea unworkable. Then came Arkus-Duntov's team, who placed a Mk IV engine ahead of the rear wheels. Because the company hadn't got round to producing a decent transaxle for the rear, the engineers considered using the front-drive one used in Oldsmobile's Toronado.

For one reason or another none of these ideas got off the ground. For one thing the softened Mako Shark shape lent itself perfectly to a conventional front-engine, rear-drive configuration. Therefore the shape was dropped on the Sting Ray chassis and the car went from there. Wind-tunnel tests produced a lot of front end lift, one of the problems that kept the car from being introduced, as originally intended, as a 1967 model. The lift was solved with functional front fender louvers and a small spoiler below the grille.

The fastback design of the Mako Shark II and of course the 1963/67 Sting Ray was dropped in favor of a Targa-type roof very similar to Ferrari's Dino. This featured a

Previous pages: from any angle, the 1967 Sting Ray was a superb design that was right in either fastback or convertible form. As can be seen from the dash layout (above), nothing was left to chance, everything was thought out. It is fitting that the National Corvette Restorer's Society should hold its major concours at the beautiful Cypress Gardens Park in Florida. Both cars and gardens complement each other.

removable recessed rear window and removable tops – the first T-top had come into being. Swooping front and rear fenders plus a vee-shaped nose told of the car's shark-like heritage, and the rear ended in an abrupt vertical style with the inclusion of a small spoiler on top. Hidden windshield wipers under a vacuum operated panel, and pop-up instead of revolving headlights, also vacuum operated, would plague owners of this fifth generation Corvette for some time. For the first time there were no side vent windows; Corvette was just following the fashion of the day, but it was a feature that would never return.

Nineteen sixty-seven was the first year of the L-88 engine. This was a 430 hp motor displacing 427 cubic inches. Before discussing this engine further it might be helpful to explain the L-88 suffix. Prior to 1963 all Corvette engines were given numerals for identification coding. From 1963, however, letters and numbers were used, hence L-88 for the above mentioned engine. This is a very famous suffix in Corvette lore for it refers to an engine that came with aluminum heads, larger exhaust valves, blueprint tolerances, a single four bbl as large as a manhole cover, and balanced racing pistons. The L-88 was the nearest thing to a fully fledged racing engine and cost almost $1,000 dollars. Its rating was given as 430 horsepower. This was probably to placate edgy insurance companies, but the author has it on good authority that this engine was turning out something nearer 560 real horsepower. Only twenty were built in 1967; only three supposedly survive to this day.

The L-88 was offered in the new 1968 Corvette. Same displacement, same hp and same price. Eighty were built and there are probably a dozen or more that survive. Of all Corvettes dating from that period the L-88 optioned model is the most desirable – and the most expensive.

The standard engine was the 300 hp 327 mated to a three-speed manual, the same combination as before. Another 327 was the 350 hp V-8 which was favored by many motoring magazines. The big 427 engines started with the 390, then 400 horsepower units. Then came the infamous L-88 and two versions of the 435 horsepower job. One, the L-71, was the tamer of the two versions, while the L-71/89 was similar in some respects to the L-88. The price of the basic convertible was $4,320, and $4,663 for the coupé,. But for raw horsepower, gut-wrenching acceleration, and high top speed, the L-88 was the only way to go.

Chevrolet wanted to try the L-88 against some real opposition and where better to do this than on a race track. With tongue-in-cheek dishonesty, Chevrolet glibly told the FIA it had built 500 L-88s (500 was the number required for homologation) when it really had only built a handful. A few were sent to face the heavyweights in the car racing world and it was now the turn of the Ferraris, Maseratis, Cobras and others to run for cover. Corvette beat everything in sight. How different racing would have been had GM allowed its divisions to go into competition. There's every reason to believe Corvette would have been way out on top.

For model year 1968, 28,566 Corvettes were built – a new record. Even though there had been criticism from various sections of the motoring press, buyers didn't agree.

Nineteen sixty-seven was the Sting Ray's final year; 1968 would be an all-new model. Five seasons of improvements made this last Sting Ray the finest of the breed and today one of the most desirable collector cars of all.

1968 SPECIFICATIONS

Engine: Ohv V-8, water-cooled, cast-iron block and heads. Bore and stroke: 4.00 x 3.48. Bhp: 350 @ 5800. Compression ratio: 11.0:1. Carburetion: Rochester 4-bbl carbureter.

Chassis: Front suspension: Independent upper and lower A-arms, coil springs, tubular hydraulic shock absorbers, anti-roll bar. Rear suspension: Independent lateral leaf spring, struts, U-jointed halfshafts, trailing arms, tubular hydraulic shock absorbers. Steering: Saginaw recirculating-ball. Brakes: Vented 4-wheel discs, 11.75-in. dia.; single caliper; 461 sq. in. effective lining area. Transmission: 4-speed manual. Final drive ratio: 3.70:1.

Measurements: Weight: 3260lbs. Tire size: F70 x 15. Track: 58.3 front, 59.0 rear. Wheelbase: 98.0″ Overall length: 182.1″ Overall width: 69.2″ Overall height: 47.8″ Maximum speed: 130mph. Fuel consumption: 11-15mpg.

Of this total, 18,630 were convertibles. Unfortunately, perhaps because it was a new body, there was a serious lapse in quality control: poor paint, poor finish, leaks, and fiberglass sinkage at the front of the hood which showed a line of rivets through the surface. This would improve as time went on, but low quality such as this was inexcusable.

People really *did* like the new Corvette. In 1969 production rose to a staggering (for Corvette, anyway) 38,762 units. Strangely, convertibles were almost 6,000 units behind coupés, and this trend would continue until the convertible model was withdrawn.

By now Federal government standards had begun to take a hold; all models had sidelights and other safety-related features. Steering wheel diameter was reduced by an inch, door handles were improved for safety, instrument knobs were made of rubber and the ignition switch was moved from the dash to the side of the steering column. On the exterior the word "Sting Ray" in script was placed above the front fender side louvers. Flat, push-down type door handles were located on the top of the leading edge of the doors.

Engines for 1969 were much as before; 116 L-88s were built and only two of what was described as a Special 427. Priced at $3,000 the engine, coded ZL1, was built for racing expert McLaren, who entered Corvettes in an assault on the Can-Am series. The engine was all aluminum and was by no stretch of the imagination a benevolent cruiser. Those wishing to order this engine for the street lost all the refinements one normally found in a Corvette. Air conditioning, heater, power steering and automatic transmission (Turbo-Hydramatic three-speed replaced Powerglide in 1968), all were deleted and it was mandatory to have the stiffest suspension and heavy-duty brakes. The same was true for the L-88 option.

The 327 was finally dumped in favor of a new 350-cubic-inch motor. This developed 300 hp and was standard. Remember the famous 283/283? Well, Chevrolet did it again, although perhaps not many people noticed. This time it was 350 cid rated at 350 horses, the combination lasting only two years, and was a $131.65 option. This small black powerhouse was listed for 1969 but didn't appear until 1970. Some of the many options included tilt-telescope steering, Positraction, red line tires and a four-speed heavy-duty manual transmission.

Some liked it, some didn't, but here it was: the 1968 Corvette. This version (previous pages and right) has the rare L88 engine option. Only 80 were built in 1968; fewer than a dozen survive. The L88 was a racing engine that was rated at 560 bhp! Bill Mitchell's liking for sharks is clearly visible from the full frontal view (right).

Another decade gone; what would the seventies bring? For Corvette a staggering drop in sales, down from almost 39,000 units to only 17,316. Not only Corvette but all cars of a sporting persuasion were affected. The muscle car boom was almost over, the victim of inexperienced drivers, sky-high insurance rates and government mandates. John DeLorean got on the bandwagon too. Now Chevrolet General Manager (he had been with Pontiac before replacing Ed Cole), DeLorean liked cars but was a corporation man. He considered the Corvette to be a specialist car for specialist people who would pay anything to obtain what they wanted. So he raised 1970 prices over $4,000 to $5,192 (coupé) and $4,849 (convertible). Perhaps he was right; by 1976 the cost of a base Corvette had risen to $7,604.85 and 46,588 were produced.

Cross-hatch side vents, a macho-looking exhaust shape, wider fender flares behind the wheels and a cross-hatch grille were 1970's most important exterior changes. In view of the still terrible quality control that blighted this otherwise excellent automobile it is unlikely that anyone wanted to alter the body design. A deluxe interior package was added to the option list and boasted lots of flimsy plastic wood on the dashboard and door panels. Genuine leather seats assuaged the lack of class which European journalists always gleefully point to when comparing cars from Italy, England and Germany with American-built products.

Sales started to increase again in 1971; Corvette's output was 21,801, much to Chevrolet's relief. As for the car, it was almost identical to the 1970 model, GM having decided it was more important to concentrate on reducing octane requirements as the "Feds" encroached even further on the automakers' doorstep. Engine line-up stayed as before, with variations of the 350 and 454 cid units numbering six. One, the 350 cid engine rated at 330 hp, was coded ZR-1. This was part of a racing option package and included the LT-1 engine with its solid lifters and extreme cam timing. Aluminum radiator, heavy-duty four-speed transmission and stiffer suspension components completed this $1,010 deal. Only eight were made; anybody who has one has a very special Corvette, indeed. If the "normal" LT-1 acceleration is anything to go by (0-60 in 6 seconds), the ZR-1 should have been even better.

By 1972 it was a case of the blind leading the blind for America's motor industry. The muscle car was dead, prices were rising and all heart appeared to have gone out of the industry as it wrestled with safety and emissions controls demanded by the government.

While Corvette was above most of the shenanigans taking place in the world, there was nothing it could do about government regulations regarding emissions, low-octane fuel requirements and all the other problems facing it. It was the last Corvette to feature a removable back window, a cross-hatch grille and more important, the last to offer the LT-1 350 small block with solid lifters. In 1983 the LT-1 was succeeded by the L-82 350 rated at 250 hp. This engine employed hydraulic lifters and cost half the price.

Five mph impact bumpers on the front was the government's decree for '73 and Corvette solved the problem better than most. Instead of a nose-heavy chrome bar standing six inches ahead of the rest of the car, Corvette's engineers and designers wrapped a steel bumper in deformable plastic urethane. The bumper itself

Engines were carry-overs from 1967 and the car shown right and previous pages is equipped with the small block 327 rated at 300 bhp. Many thought the small blocks ideal for the Corvette because their size and weight gave better handling and ride. The 1968 car had nice lines and a design that would last fourteen years!

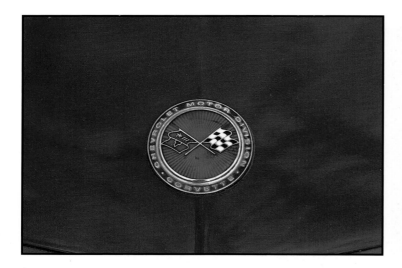

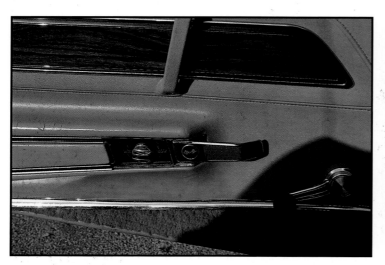

1970 SPECIFICATIONS

Engine: Ohv V-8, water-cooled, cast-iron block and heads. Bore and stroke: 4.25 x 4.00. Bhp: 390 @ 4800. Compression ratio: 10.25:1. Carburetion: Rochester 4-bbl carbureter.
Chassis: Front suspension: Independent upper and lower A-arms, coil springs, tubular hydraulic shock absorbers, anti-roll bar. Rear suspension: Independent lateral leaf spring, struts, U-jointed halfshafts, trailing arms, tubular hydraulic shock absorbers. Steering: Saginaw recirculating-ball, (power-assisted steering). Brakes: Vented 4-wheel discs, 11.75-in. dia.; single caliper; 461 sq. in. effective lining area. Transmission: 4-speed manual. 3-speed automatic. Final drive ratio: 3.08:1.
Measurements: Weight: N/A. Tire size: 205 x 15. Track: 58.7 front, 59.4 rear. Wheelbase: 98.0" Overall length: 182.5" Overall width: 69.0" Overall height: 47.4" Maximum speed: 145mph. Fuel consumptiomn: 8-12mpg.

1974 SPECIFICATIONS

Engine: Ohv V-8, water-cooled, cast-iron block and heads. Bore and stroke: 4.00 x 3.48. Bhp: 250 @ 5200. Compression ratio: 9.0:1. Carburetion: Rochester 4-bbl carbureter.
Chassis: Front suspension: Independent upper and lower A-arms, coil springs, tubular hydraulic shock absorbers, anti-roll bar. Rear suspension: Independent lateral leaf spring, struts, U-jointed halfshafts, trailing arms, tubular hydraulic shock absorbers. Steering: Saginaw recirculating-ball, (power-assisted steering). Brakes: Vented 4-wheel discs, 11.75-in. dia.; single caliper; 461 sq. in. effective lining area. Transmission: 4-speed manual. Final drive ratio: 3.70:1.
Measurements: Weight: N/A. Tire size: GR70 x 15. Track: 58.7 front, 59.5 rear. Wheelbase: 98.0" Overall length: 185.5" Overall width: 69.0" Overall height: 47.8" Maximum speed: 124mph. Fuel consumption: 12-15mpg.

A new version of the crossed flags motif (top) graced the front end and the emblem appeared in miniature on the interior door handles (above) in this 1973 model. The Stingray (top right) nomenclature became one word and was used through 1978.

was fitted to shock absorbers that would push in then pop out in the event of a mild fender bender. The urethane cover was painted body color but Corvette, like other car makers, weren't able to quite match the colors. Urethane reacts differently from fiberglass and steel so it would be some years before a solution was found.

All things considered, the '73 Corvette, America's only sports car, wasn't the happiest looking automobile. The urethane front end was well executed but it didn't match the rear, which retained its flimsy chrome excuses for bumpers for another season.

The new bumpers added 35 lbs to the overall weight of the Corvette and the sound-deadening material, liberally sprayed on many inner panels in the interests of noise abatement, probably added a few pounds more. Another improvement was the deletion of the troublesome windshield wiper door, and a new hood facilitated the improvement. Would you believe that radial tires were offered only for the first time in 1973? Compared with the old bias-belt tires, the disadvantages of the early radials were longer stopping distances and poorer over-the-road performance. Both Goodyear and Firestone only gave the new tires a 120 mph speed rating. The advantages, however, were longer life, more stability and better cornering properties.

The 1974 Corvette underwent a styling revision at the rear, with the inclusion of 5 mph impact bumpers wrapped in body color plastic urethane. A curiosity not really explained was why the rear urethane section was two piece instead of one, like the front. A line ran up the middle and if, as often occurred, the two pieces didn't match, the resemblance to a cheap Hong Kong toy springs to mind.

Buyers probably didn't know it, but 1974 was the last

1977 SPECIFICATIONS

Engine: Ohv V-8, water-cooled, cast-iron block and heads. Bore and stroke: 4.00 x 3.48. Bhp: 210 @ 5200. Compression ratio: 9.0:1. Carburetion: Rochester 4-bbl carbureter.

Chassis: Front suspension: Independent upper and lower A-arms, coil springs, tubular hydraulic shock absorbers, anti-roll bar. Rear suspension: Independent lateral leaf spring, struts, U-jointed halfshafts, trailing arms, tubular hydraulic shock absorbers. Steering: Saginaw recirculating-ball, (power-assisted steering). Brakes: Vented 4-wheel discs, 11.75-in. dia.; single caliper; 461 sq. in. effective lining area. Transmission: 4-speed manual. Final drive ratio: 3.70:1.

Measurements: Weight: 3450lbs. Tire size: GR70 x 15. Track: 58.7 front, 59.5 rear. Wheelbase: 98.0" Overall length: 185.2" Overall width: 70.0" Overall height: 48.0" Maximum speed: N/A. Fuel consumption: 13-16mpg.

year for the 454 engine – all that would be left from 1970 on would be the 350. There was a s yet no catalytic converter, but that would come in 1975. Dual exhausts would run into one, flow through the converter, then divide on the other side. The HEI or High Energy Ignition system would also make its debut in 1975. This would offer a vast improvement over the transistorized system used since 1965. As far as engine power went, well, it went! By 1975 the base 350 put out a puny 165 bhp. the L-82 was the only option and that only wheezed 205 bhp.

These figures reflect net horsepower, not gross, as before. When Ed Cole became President of GM, he still kept abreast of what was happening within each car division. Then he announced that from 1971 all horsepower figures would be SAE net – that is with all accessories fitted to the engine. The old figures were gross horsepower – or before any accessories were added. SAE is a far more honest appraisal of horsepower because the figures represent over-the-road maximums. Therefore 165 and 205 bhp don't look quite as bad as if the figures had been arrived at on a dynamometer.

Nineteen seventy-five was the last year until 1986 for a Corvette convertible. The urethane rear bumper cover became a one-piece unit, better impact-absorbent materials forming its inner core. The number of units produced marched upwards: 33,836 coupés and only 4,629 convertibles. No wonder Chevrolet dumped the convertible!

July 4th, 1976 and America was 200 years old. Great celebrations were held across the nation, yet oddly no car maker brought out a special limited, bi-centennial edition, not even Corvette. The way things were, it was unlikely the motor industry felt like celebrating, for it was suffering a great depression of the corporate mind, quality was in the doldrums and so were most of the cars. Corvette stayed much the same, with just a little trim fiddling to suffice. One bit of good news was the increase in horsepower for both engines: the 165 went to 180 horsepower and the 205 was increased by five horses, to 210.

In its ninth year with the same body, Corvette didn't show any signs of changing, and a policy of constant improvement and refinement was the order of the day – or should we say years? A new interior, the first since 1968, was the catch-all for 1977, the year in which leather seats became standard in Corvettes, and cars with automatic transmission were offered cruise-control for the first time. As for engines, the two 350s were the same as in 1976. Production rose to 49,213 and the price had sky-rocketed over $1,000 since 1976, to $8,647.65, thanks to general inflation and escalating oil costs.

Elegant silver on gray paintwork distinguishes the silver anniversary edition that celebrated 25 years of Corvette.

Although there had been no special edition to mark the nation's two-hundredth birthday, in 1978 Corvette rolled out two specials of its own. One was Corvette's Silver Anniversary Edition to celebrate the 25th birthday of America's only sports car. Additionally, to commemorate the choice of a Corvette as pace car for the Indianapolis 500 that year, a limited edition Pace Car Corvette was unveiled. Two special editions in one year!

Distinctive two-tone black over silver paint separated by a red pinstripe, new thin-shell buckets upholstered in either silver leather or silver and gray cloth with gray carpets, distinguished the Pace Car. Red "Official Pace Car" lettering, part of an Indy 500 decal package, was included with the car but not factory installed; the dealer would do this if the owner so wished. New glass T-tops, anti-theft package, aluminum wheels, tilt-telescope steering, power windows, power locks, power brakes, air conditioning, eight track tape player (or CB radio), AM/FM stereo, rear defogger and other bits and pieces, all were standard in the Pace Car replica. Power was provided by Corvette's only optional engine, now rated at 220 bhp. At what cost, one may ask. $13,653.21 was $4,302 more than the ordinary Corvette and actually almost $1,000 more for all the add-ons than if one had bought a plain Jane Corvette and ordered the pieces oneself. Only 2,500 units had been planned, but fearing lest some of the 6,200 dealers would feel left out, Chevrolet decided that one be built for each dealer. So the Pace Car wasn't very "limited" after all.

Nor was the Silver Anniversary Edition, either. Any Corvette could become a Silver Anniversary car because Corvette offered a "25th Anniversary Paint" package of silver over gray, again separated by a pinstripe. Options included in this package were the aluminum wheels and dual door

mirrors, otherwise it was just another Corvette. All 1978 models carried a special silver medallion replete with red and checkered crossed flags, the number "25" above the flags and "Corvette – 1953 Anniversary 1978" round the perimeter.

The following year saw more of the same, but without special edition packages. The L-82 optional 350 V-8 crept up to 225 bhp, the base L-48 to 195. Bolt-on front and rear spoilers, as used on the 1978 Pace Car, were offered on all 1979 Corvettes as an option as wind-tunnel tests had proved that spoilers reduced drag by up to fifteen percent. In layman terms this meant an additional half mile per gallon of gas. With Corporate Average Fuel Economy (CAFE) measures breathing down car makers' necks, even a thimble full of gas saved was something to be proud about. Sticker price of the '79 zoomed almost $1,000, to $10,220.23 for a base Corvette, but AM/FM became standard radio equipment! Since 1974 Corvette prices had jumped $4,219, yet 1979 production posted a new record, with 53,807 built.

Another decade was wrapped up and put away for historians to ponder over in years to come. There had been numerous changes at Corvette; Zora Arkus-Duntov had retired at the end of 1974, and Bill Mitchell in 1977; Ed Cole retired during the seventies and Harley Earl had gone in the sixties – four men whose faith and enthusiasm had guaranteed Corvette a permanent place in American motoring legend; four men who are the soul of an American institution.

Changes for 1978 included new fastback roofline with wraparound rear window. The Silver Anniversary Edition was mostly cosmetics at an inflated price. Quality was lacking, as shown by the ragged carpet edge (facing page top) and poor door fit (facing page bottom right).

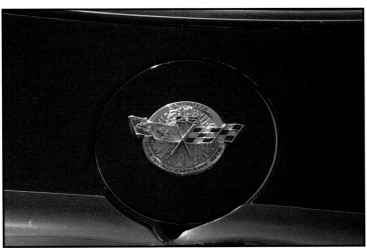

1978 CORVETTE COUPE L48 350 V8 INDY PACE CAR

CHAPTER FIVE
THE ULTIMATE AMERICAN
PERFORMANCE CAR

For all the emissions controls and the extra weight added by safety features, the Corvette could still perform well. Perhaps not as fast as before, but *Car and Driver* tested a 1979 model with the L-82 engine and ran a 0-60 time in 6.6 seconds. Top speed was recorded at 127 mph. Mindful that weight means poor economy, Corvette shed 250 lbs. for 1980, partly through building the differential housing and front-frame crossmember out of aluminum instead of steel. Depressingly, more plastics were used throughout, and especially in the interior. Plastic saves weight, cuts down costs and is safer than steel to the human frame; but does a Corvette interior have to have the look of a basic Cavalier? The trouble with plastic is its uniformity, which makes the interiors of a $100,000 or $10,000 car look the same.

Another oil crisis was precipitated by the overthrow of the Shah of Iran; inflation in America was on a runaway course, and Chrysler Corporation, at death's door, asked the federal government for a $1 billion loan. Lee Iacocca, recently and mysteriously fired from Ford, took over as President of Chrysler. B-movie actor Ronald Reagan was elected President of the United States. As for the 1980 Corvette, it was given new front and rear bumper "cover," both with integral spoilers built in. Air conditioning became standard, as did tilt-telescope steering. And even if your Corvette – or any U.S.-built car, for that matter – could turn in a respectable speed, you wouldn't know because another government decree allowed speedometers to be calibrated only to 85 mph.

Even with the so-called hard times and a $13,140 base price 40,614 Corvettes were built. In 1981 its price rose to an alarming $16,258.52, yet 40,606 units left two plants. Production was being scaled down to nothing at St. Louis, while the brand-new high-tech Corvette plant at Bowling Green, Kentucky, began to take on production. Quite a large number of the St. Louis workers were relocated to Bowling Green and rumors abounded that an all-new Corvette would soon be announced.

Certainly it was time for a new model, for the 1981 car was becoming old hat. Sports cars have to advance – in a sense they are test beds for future family cars. The Corvette in its then current form had outlived its usefulness; after all it was thirteen years old. For some reason Chevrolet was never able to cure the quality control problems that had plagued Corvette since 1968. It was so bad that one major car journal refused to test a Corvette due to the appalling quality. By the mid-seventies it had got so bad that quality was the first thing car testers looked for – but rarely found. Imagine the guffaws had this been a Yugo or some other East European car.

Computer Command Control (CCC) was Corvette's newsmaker in 1981. This electronics device was used to modulate ignition timing and air/fuel mixtures in order to reduce emissions and fuel consumption. The automatic transmission had a new lock-up torque converter clutch, a standard quartz clock was part of the increasingly luxurious

Selected as the Indianapolis Pace Car for 1978, Corvette had two special editions that year. Demand for both was great, with greedy dealers asking as much as $28,000 for one. Even uglier was the profusion of phony Limited Editions that turned up. The ones illustrated are all genuine.

*Thin shell leather buckets and all silver interior (top) distinguish
the Pace Car replica. The spoiler (above) was an exclusive
addition. Two-tone paint on the Silver Anniversary and Pace Car
models was the first such on a Corvette.*

1982 SPECIFICATIONS

Engine: Ohv V-8 water-cooled, cast-iron block and heads. Bore and stroke: 4.00 x 3.48. Bhp: 200 @ 4200. Compression ratio: 9.0:1. Carburetion: GM 'Cross-Fire' dual throttle-body fuel injection.
Chassis: Front suspension: Independent upper and lower A-arms, coil springs, tubular hydraulic shock absorbers, anti-roll bar. Rear suspension: Independent lower lateral arms, axle halfshafts as upper lateral arms, trailing arms, transverse leaf spring, tubular shock absorbers, anti-roll bar. Steering: Saginaw power-assisted recirculating-ball. Brakes: 11.75-in. Ventilated discs; front and rear; 461 sq. in. effective lining area. Transmission: 4-speed automatic. Final drive ratio: 2.87:1
Measurements: Weight: 3425lbs. Tire size: P255 x 60R-15. Goodyear Eagle GT. Track: 58.7 front, 59.5 rear. Wheelbase: 98.0" Overall length: 185.3" Overall width: 69.0" Overall height: 48.4" Maximum speed: 125mph. Fuel consumption: 19-21mpg.

interior, and a six-way power driver's seat was a new option. The last Corvette to be built at the St. Louis factory, No. 1G1AY8764BS431611, was completed on August 1st, 1981. Perhaps somebody has this car without realizing it.

It was official: a new Corvette was in the wings and would soon be introduced. Therefore the 1982 model was the last of the line that stretched back to 1968, its chassis to 1963. As if to celebrate the fact, a special Collector's Edition was produced. Power output of the venerable 350 was 200, but the big news was a return to fuel injection with "Cross-Fire Injection"– a system quite different from that which had been used on 1957-65 cars. An injector unit within the throttle body dealt with each cylinder bank. This was an extremely efficient system which, coupled to the CCC electronics, was probably one of the best fuel injection arrangements on any car.

A unique VIN plate was incorporated in the new model to help prevent the appearance of bogus "Collector Editions" as had happened with the limited edition 1978 Pace Car replica. The 6,759 examples that were produced were made only to order, and with a tag of $22,537.59, it is surprising that so many were made. Price for the base Corvette was now $18,290.07.

So, what did the buyer get for his $22,537 – not forgetting the fifty-nine cents? A smart paint job of metallic silver with graduated gray striping that started at the front fender louver and swept back in an ever lightening hue to the rear of the door. This same treatment was applied to the hood as well. Bronze tint glass T-tops, finned alloy wheels reminiscent of those first seen on the 1963 model, and a rear window that opened up like a hatchback. Silver-beige leather upholstery, door trim and leather-wrapped steering wheel. Cloisonne emblems on hood, rear and steering wheel completed the visual differences. Of course the car was loaded, but there was only a single transmission choice in 1982. All Corvettes came fitted with a four-speed automatic.

From 1968 to 1982 the years had comprised a story of growth and development, and now the fifth generation Corvette, like a dowager duchess, took its bow and left the stage. Even with its bad assembly, decreasing performance and outrageous pricing, the old Corvette had many loyal friends who loved the cars. Perhaps its imperfections added to its charisma – after all, a perfect car becomes a boring car.

Another special Corvette, this time the 1982 Collector Edition. The car was in its fourteenth year and there was little more designers could do to improve it. The nose had, over the years, taken on Cyrano de Bergerac proportions, but it was still quite an attractive car. Only 6,759 Collector Editions were built, and the car had its own ID plates to foil forgers.

Work on the 1984 sixth generation Corvette had begun during 1978, and for a while there had been talk of a mid-engined model called the Aerovette. At one point it was approved for production in 1980 but was killed off for various reasons. One of those reasons was David R. McLellan, Zora Arkus-Duntov's successor. McLellan preferred the front/mid engine layout as opposed to the rear/mid engine design. The idea was shelved and work started on the shape of things to come.

David McLellan was chief engineer and Jerry Palmer led the design team. The brief was to design a car as competitive as any other modern sports car, bring about a better quality program and make the Corvette one of the best-handling cars in the world. In the beginning most of these qualities were reached, though there were reservations regarding handling and, later, quality control.

Chevrolet invited all the magazines and press people to Riverside Raceway in southern California for the unveiling of the new Corvette on November 30th, 1982. Expectantly the various elements representing the media waited; finally the car was given an enthusiastic response from all. The same reaction, perhaps even more favorable, was displayed in Chevrolet showrooms across the country when the new Corvette went on sale in the spring of 1983 as a 1984 model. It was odd, however, that considering it was the car's thirteenth birthday that year there was no 1983 model. Perhaps Chevrolet thought the new model celebration enough.

As far as the new shape went, it was as different from previous Corvettes as chalk is from cheese. Nevertheless, there was a family resemblance somewhere, for there was no mistaking the car for anything other than a Corvette. The new design was aerodynamically pure, the front sniffing

The Collector Edition's plush interior (top) seemed more in keeping with luxury cars rather than Corvette, but the vaned wheels (above) are a nice touch. The rear of the Corvette is simple yet stylish, even though the letters spelling out "Corvette" are a shade overdone. The 350 cid engine put out 200 SAE hp and "Cross-fire injection" refers to GM's fuel injection system.

the ground like an ant-eater, the flush-fitted windshield huge in depth and raked back as far as the designers dared. Such was the new Corvette styling that one could almost see the wind flowing over its lines in a clean sweep.

The wheelbase had been chopped two inches to 96 and the overall length came down from 185.3 to 176.5, but width was increased to 71 inches – two inches more than the 1982 model. Weight dropped by 245 lbs to 3,200lbs, still quite heavy compared to some.

A unitized steel/aluminum integral perimeter-birdcage formed the structure around which the Corvette was built. This was the first time Corvette had abandoned body-on-frame in favor of unitary construction, but the advantages included a more rigid platform, tighter assembly and much improved handling. This was achieved by McLellan's team taking the familiar front suspension consisting of unequal length upper and lower A-arms, and replacing the old coil springs with a single reinforced transversely mounted fiberglass leaf spring. A 20 mm anti-roll bar and tubular hydraulic shock absorbers took care of the rest.

At the rear, Zora Arkus-Duntov s old three-link suspension gave way to a five-link arrangement: upper and lower trailing arms, lateral arms, and twin lateral strut rods which attached the differential to the hub carriers. Again a transverse fiberglass leaf spring was used. U-jointed half-shafts and rear tie rods, hydraulic shocks and an anti-roll bar completed a very sophisticated picture.

The birdcage frame comprised windshield and door frames, rocker panels, lower A-pillar extensions and the front sub-frame. The fiberglass panels were mated to the frame to give exceptional strength as well as safety for driver and passenger. Huge sixteen-inch wheels were shod in Goodyear Eagle VR-50s. These tires were clearly a development of the Goodyear Formula One program. It was this and other Goodyear competition adventures that bore fruit to create the Corvette's tires.

Rack and pinion steering with a quite fast 15.5:1 ratio and overall better precision and control replaced the old recirculating ball system. Four-wheel disc brakes were made for Corvette by Girlock of Australia and boasted a 184-square-inch lining area. A four-speed manual and four-speed automatic were available, though the first cars were built with automatics. The four-speed unit was called "4 plus 3 overdrive." This was a normal four-speed unit with the provision of three overdrive gears. These planetary gears were activated by the CCC through a hydraulic clutch and provided an overdrive reduction in each of the top three gears. This clever little trick improved fuel economy, always a bugbear when developing sports cars.

Under the hood (the whole front end swung forward for easy access to the engine) was the old 350 ohv V-8 rated at 205 horsepower. Performance was good: 0-60 in 7 seconds and a top speed of 140 mph, with fuel consumption an excellent 16 to 20 mpg.

People packaging had been much improved, with more space on the inside, better located seats and controls. A tilt-telescope steering wheel was standard and options included leather seating surfaces and a Delco-Bose stereo system. The back window opened up like a hatch, a feature carried over from the 1982 Collector Edition. As for the instruments, these were a colorful display board of graphic analog and digital readouts. For those who wanted the

Here was class, world class, in the shape of the beautiful new 1984 Corvette. This sixth generation Corvette had been a long time in coming, but one look tells us the wait was more than worth it.

1984
SPECIFICATIONS

Engine: Ohv V-8 water-cooled, cast-iron block and heads. Bore and stroke: 4.00 x 3.48. Bhp: 205 @ 4300. Compression ratio: 9.0:1. Carburetion: GM 'Cross-Fire' dual throttle-body fuel injection.

Chassis: Front suspension: Independent; unequal-length upper and lower A-arms, transverse fiberglass leaf spring, tubular hydraulic shock absorbers, anti-roll bar. Rear suspension: Independent; upper and lower trailing arms, lateral arms, tie rods, halfshafts, transverse fiberglass leaf spring, tubular hydraulic shock absorbers, anti-roll bars. Steering: Power assisted rack-and-pinion. Brakes: 4-wheel ventilated discs, 11.5-in. dia.; 184 sq. in effective lining area. Transmission: 4-speed automatic. Final drive ratio: 3.31:1.

Measurements: Weight: 3200lbs. Tire size: Goodyear Eagle. VR50, P255/50VR-16. Track: 59.6 front, 60.4 rear. Wheelbase: 96.2″ Overall length: 176.5″ Overall width: 71.0″ Overall height: 46.7″ Maximum speed: 140mph. Fuel consumption: 16-20mpg.

If you were a truck driver, the view shown facing page might be one of the few you would get of the Corvette, although most motorists would have seen the tail (above). Right: Corvette returned to single headlights for the first time since 1958.

131

luxury, special seats could be ordered with lumbar support, backrest angle and cushion bolster. By pressing buttons and squeezing pumps one could theoretically find the perfect seating position. Unfortunately, those on the corpulent side would not be able to sit in either standard or special Corvette seats.

Corvette's engineers had set out to build a sports car with handling properties approaching the best in the world. This they accomplished, but at a price. From *Consumer Guide* to *Motor Trend*, all the testers complained about the bone-jarring ride. The suspension was so stiff that even the smallest bump in the road resembled driving over railroad sleepers. "... stiff and jarring on patchy surfaces." moaned *Consumer Guide*, who also complained about the noise level. The problem was that the suspension had been designed to emulate a racing car on the corners and the ride had been forgotten.

Was it a good car for the $21,800 that the base model cost? For road-hugging performance, yes; for cornering at speeds never before thought possible in a road-going car, yes; for a summer evening cruise into the country, no. Yet neither the criticism nor the price put off the buyers, who lined up in droves, completed loan applications in hand, and bought 51,547 of the new model – more than double the 25,407 produced in 1982. All the journals agreed that the '84 Corvette was a world-class sports car, but, as *Consumer Guide* put it "...you have to live with a bump and grind ride and plenty of noise to enjoy it."

Sensible economics, public awareness about the oil situation and people buying smaller, more fuel-efficient cars had produced an oil glut in the world. Gas prices came tumbling down and the economy was booming. Performance cars were having a renaissance by the mid-eighties, but sophisticated cars with sometimes four-cylinder turbocharged engines that could go as quickly as the old "brute force and ignorance" machinery of the sixties were being developed. In addition, there was more money around. Corvette's price hikes proved that. More people were buying expensive luxury and sporty imports regardless of cost. Ferrari was readying a new limited edition GTO and a production Testarossa at prices that would make the Corvette's pale into insignificance, and in 1985 Corvette dropped Cross-Fire Injection and introduced "Turned Point Injection" instead.

Basically the German Bosch system, TPI featured a mass airflow sensor, aluminum tube-tuned runners, a plenum and an air cleaner perched forward of the radiator support. Incoming air is collected in the plenum sitting on top of the engine. The tuned runners curve out from the plenum, run beneath it to individual intake ports and pile up air above each port, ramming it into the combustion chamber when the intake valves open.

Because of the criticisms arriving daily at Bowling Green with regard to the too-stiff suspension, Chevrolet's engineers worked hard to improve the ride without losing handling. The 1985 models consequently had softer spring and shock rates for the standard suspension as well as the Z51 performance option package. Other improvements included removing annoying squeaks and rattles that plagued the '84 models. This was mostly a quality control problem.

Corvette offered a convertible in 1986, the first for eleven years. Selected to pace the 1986 Indy 500, Corvette decided all 1986 convertibles would be Indy 500 Pace Car Replicas. Although the Pace Car was painted a new shade of yellow, buyers were given a choice of colors along with a complete set of decals to stick on the car if so desired. The owner of this "Replica" decided not to take up the offer.

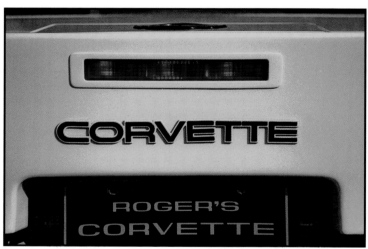

Top: rear mirrors are standard on both sides and are operated electrically. Above center: location of the parking brake lever is unconventional and reminiscent of Bentleys and Stutz. Above: Federal law dictated a new brake light in 1986 and Corvette found the most satisfactory location for it. Right: even painted taxi cab yellow, the Corvette is very svelte, very sexy.

1988 SPECIFICATIONS

Engine: Ohv V-8, water-cooled; cast-iron block, aluminum heads. Bore and stroke: 4.00 x 3.48. Bhp: 245 @ 4300. Compression ratio: 9.0:1. Carburetion: Bosch multi-port fueling.
Chassis: Front suspension: Independent; unequal-length upper and lower A-arms, transverse fiberglass leaf spring, tubular hydraulic shock absorbers, anti-roll bar. Rear suspension: Independent; upper and lower trailing arms, lateral arms, tie rods, halfshafts, transverse fiberglass leaf spring, tubular hydraulic shock absorbers, anti-roll bars. Steering: Power-assisted rack-and-pinion, 15 x 5:1 standard ratio (13.0:1 with Z51/Z52 handling packages). Brakes: 4-wheel ventilated discs, 11.5-in. dia.; Bosch ABS II 3-channel anti-lock braking system; 184 sq. in. effective lining area. Transmission: '4 + 3' overdrive manual. 4-speed overdrive automatic. Final drive ratio: 2.59:1/2.73:1 std. coupe/convertible; 3.07:1 optional.
Measurements: Weight: 3298-3333lbs. Tire size: Goodyear Eagle ZR50, P255/50ZR-16 (P275/40ZR-17 with optional Z51 and Z52 handling packages). Track: 59.6 front, 60.4 rear. Wheelbase: 96.2" Overall length: 176.5" Overall width: 71.0" Overall height: 46.7" coupe, 46.4" convertible. Maximum speed: 154mph. Fuel consumption: 14-18mpg.

Tests proved the engineers were on the right track, for the suspension was vastly improved, particularly the standard version. One magazine waxed lyrical over the improvement and said the 150-mph car was so good it "… makes your heart soar." The engine was now rated at 230 bhp and could propel the Corvette to 60 in 5.7 seconds.

Sales dropped to 39,729 in 1985, probably due to another exorbitant price hike. People will only take so much for so long, and a more critical public was noting Corvette's quality was lamentably poor compared to foreign imports. Chevrolet had added a further $3,000 to the price since the year before, and would do so again in 1986.

The return of the convertible in 1986 was welcome, as was the introduction of ABS braking. This particular anti-lock system came from Bosch and was similar to that used by Mercedes and BMW. A new anti-theft device was also employed as standard and was quite a deterrent to would-be car thieves. As for the convertible, this model was selected as the official 1986 Indy Pace Car. As before, Chevrolet supplied decals that the dealer could put on if a new owner so wished.

By the end of the year, 7,315 convertibles and 27,794 coupés had been built. Now the coupé cost $27,502, but the convertible was a ridiculous $32,507. Looking at what Corvette did in 1987 we see that prices were up again – were they never satisfied? A coupé was up to $28,474; the convertible to $33,647. Maybe it was to help recoup the money GM had spent buying British sports car manufacturer Lotus in 1986, whose purchase would prove to be significant in the next couple of years. There was another increase in horsepower, this time to 240, and engines now had aluminum cylinder heads. These were introduced in 1986, but problems with cracks appearing round the attachment points delayed full-scale production until the trouble was eliminated.

Into 1988 and the new Corvettes were basically refinements of what went before. Suspension was being continually upgraded to eliminate the horrors of 1984, while to celebrate Corvette's birthday, a 35th Anniversary

Decked out and ready to race, and that's exactly what this impressive looking 1988 Corvette (previous pages and right) was built for. The Corvette Challenge Series, begun in 1987, was the brainchild of John Powell. He created the series in response to criticism from other sports car manufacturers who complained that Corvettes always won SCCA events and that they had an unfair advantage. Sanctioned by the SCCA, the Challenge Series was a set of races for Corvettes only.

Corvette's Bowling Green, Kentucky, plant built the special Challenge Series cars, the engines were sealed to prevent any tampering, and the driver sat within a strong safety cage. In 1987 100 Challenge Corvettes were built, 50 in 1988 and 1989, the last year of the series before the SCCA modified its rules and Corvettes once again challenged the rest of the world. The car pictured here was the overall winner of the 1988 Challenge Series. Tom Bell's team is rumored to have picked up a million dollars for winning the series.

Edition was offered. Its appearance was that of a visiting angel: all white, as pure as the driven snow – white body, white wheels, white leather upholstery, white door panels and white steering wheel. Naturally it was loaded with sophisticated gadgetry. The hot gossip going round wherever car people gathered was of Corvette's ultimate car currently being tested and planned for February 1989 introduction. This was to be the ZR-1.

Corvette needed a boost such as the ZR-1 to help stem flagging sales, because by the end of 1988 only 22,789 had been sold, and the sixth generation Corvette wasn't selling in the volume that the fifth generation car had done. So the ZR-1 would be a welcome boost. Selected journalists were invited to the Milford Proving Grounds to see the car, which on first sight looked like any other sixth generation red Corvette. Wait a minute! There *was* something different. The rear end was wider by at least three inches and the taillights were oval instead of being circular.

The reason for the extra rear width was to enable Chevy engineers to cram huge Goodyear Eagle Gatorbacks, measuring 315/35ZR17. Almost 12.5 inches wide, the tires lay three inches more rubber on the blacktop than the standard Corvette, thus adding greatly to the car's handling and performance. This was extremely important because Chevrolet was aiming for not only the best-handling car in the world but also one of the fastest.

Lotus, that charismatic little sports car firm nestled in the flatlands of England, was the company responsible for hordes of Formula One winners. The company had helped create the fabulous British Ford Lotus-Cortina and was responsible for the legendary Elite, Elan, Europa and Espirit. From its very beginning, in the days of its founder, the late Colin Chapman, all Lotus production cars have been manufactured from fiberglass. In the spring of 1985 GM management entered into discussions with Lotus managing director Tony Rudd with a view to buying the company outright. During this time Corvette engineers were discussing the viability of adapting Lotus' four-valve head to the Corvette's 350 V-8. Rudd thought differently. How about an all-new engine? This is precisely what Corvette engineering chief David McLellan, and Chevy chief engineer Fred Schaafsma wanted to hear. Neither one was happy with the current state of affairs. Here was the Corvette, a world-class sports car and yet its powerplant, the ohv 350 V-8, was almost as antiquated as the original Blue Flame Six!

After successful discussions, Lotus became a wholly owned GM subsidiary in 1986. All the while talks had been going on, Messrs. McLellan and Schaafsma had been prodding and pestering the management to let the Corvette have a new engine. Once the takeover had been approved the engineers got their way and were able to work with Lotus to produce a new engine.

The result was the 32 valve, or four valves per cylinder, twin overhead cam all-aluminum V-8. It displaced 350 cubic inches (5.7 liters) and developed 380 bhp, while Tuned Port Injection (TPI) took care of the engine's fuel needs. An interesting development concerning engine power is located at the base of the console to the left of the shifter, where a key is inserted into what looks like an ignition switch. Turn it to the left where it says "Normal" or turn it to the right where it says "Full". If the key is left in the

Nineteen eighty-eight was the 35th anniversary of Corvette's birth, and a special edition was created to celebrate the event. Equipped with the 17-inch wheels that Corvette had introduced in 1988, the Special Edition came only in coupé form and was clothed in white even down to the wheels.

Above: the tried and true 350 cid OHV V8, which developed 245 horsepower in 1988, reposes under the Tuned Port Injection system. Left: part of the dash display showing air conditioning and radio/cassette controls. Facing page: the only dark surfaces on the exterior of the 35th Anniversary Edition are the windows, glass roof and low-profile Goodyears, The white leather covered steering wheel (bottom left) may be in questionable taste, but the rear window (bottom right) serves as a sensible hatch to a small luggage area.

normal mode, the engine's power is relegated to 200; should you wish to find out what happens when the position is on full, watch out. That's when the engine's full power is tapped, propelling this amazing machine up to its maximum 185 mph.

Standard suspension on the ZR-1 is the Z51 Performance Handling Package optional on normal Corvettes. To this has been added Delco-Bilstein Selective Ride Control which allows the driver to set up the suspension three ways; touring, sport and competition. The only transmission is a six-speed ZF manual unit which has very close ratios, particularly between first and third.

I recently spent some time with a 1990 Corvette ZR-1 and all I can really say is that this car is everything it is cracked up to be and more. The car had an attractive interior that is somewhat marred by the A-pillar moldings which were cheap plastic and exhibited four nasty Philips screws, two for each side. The leather seats are firm yet comfortable, and have many adjustments, including lumbar support, bolsters that tighten or lessen their grip at the touch of a button, forward, back, up or down and all done with little levers and buttons.

Originally the instrument panel was to have been digital but at the last minute this was changed to a series of traditional dials. Everything is there, right in front of the driver. To the right are the air conditioning controls and the superb Delco-Bose stereo radio and tape deck. Unfortunately Chevrolet hasn't yet succeeded in damping out the harsh noises delivered to the interior by the colossal tires, therefore one cannot really appreciate how good this radio really is. To do that would mean buying a Cadillac.

The German-built ZF six-speed manual transmission is a delight to use, the shifts smooth and positive with none of that vague slushiness exhibited by some manual boxes. There can be a problem in shifting from first to second, so that until one gets used to the close "gates" there is the possibility, or rather the probability, of missing second and ending up in fourth. Even so, there is no stalling; obviously engine revs are way down, but the car is forgiving, picks itself up and after a few seconds proceeds as if nothing had happened.

As we approach the end of the twentieth century, advanced technology has taken a lot of the fun away from us. Cars are a good example. They have become so perfect that they are blasé. Where's the thrill in driving perfection? This may sound a little crazy, especially when the ZR-1 is as close to perfection as one can get. It has something only Ferrari can possibly share: charisma. Go into the garage and there's the ZR-1, like a happy lap-dog crouching low, waiting to be taken out.

The driver's seat hugs you, holds you tight like a long lost son. Foot down on the clutch, turn the key and the engine roars to life. Not that laid-back rumbling sound of old; the note is on a higher key. You grip the gear shifter, pull up under the knob to go into reverse and back out onto the driveway. The car waits, its engine note eager with anticipation. The keyed switch above the shifter, slightly to the left, is set to normal.

Into first and the ZR-1 moves forward in a well-mannered way. The suspension is set to the touring mode. The road is quiet so let's try racing through the gears without picking

The Corvette sits upon 9.5-inch-wide wheels shod in low-profile Goodyear Eagles. The car's wind-cheating look is enhanced by the flush windshield and rounded fender peaks. Chrome, happily, is only a distant memory.

1989
SPECIFICATIONS

Engine: L98 — 90-degree ohv V-8, water-cooled. Aluminum heads and cast-iron block. (LT5 — all aluminum). Bore and stroke: L98 — 4.00 x 3.48. (LT5 — 3.90 x 3.66). Bhp: L98 — 245 @ 4300 (LT5 — N/A). Compression ratio: L98 -9.0:1 (LT5 — 11.25:1). Carburetion: Bosch multi-port fuel injection.

Chassis: Front suspension: Independent; unequal-length upper and lower A-arms, transverse fiberglass leaf spring, tubular hydraulic shock absorbers, (ZR-1 and FX3 options: variable rate via electric actuators), anti-roll bar. Rear suspension: Independent; upper and lower trailing arms, lateral arms, tie rods, halfshafts, transverse fiberglass leaf spring, tubular hydraulic shock absorbers, (ZR-1 and FX3 options: variable rate via electric actuators), anti-roll bar. Steering: Power-assisted rack-and-pinion, 13.0:1 overall ratio. Brakes: 4-wheel ventilated discs, 12.0-in. dia.; Bosch ABS II 3-channel anti-lock braking system; 198 sq. in. effective lining area. Transmission: L98 — ZF 6-speed overdrive (LT5 -GM 4-speed overdrive). Final drive ratio: Manual: 3.33:1; Automatic: 2.59:1/2.73:1 std. coupe/convertible; 3.07:1 optional.

Measurements: Weight: 3298-3333lbs. Tire size: Goodyear Eagle ZR50; P275/40 ZR-17 standard except ZR-1 (P275/40 ZR-17 front, P315/35ZR-17 rear). Track: 59.6 front, 60.4 rear. Wheelbase: 96.2″ Overall length: 176.5″ Overall width: 71.0″ (2R-1 coupe; 74.0″). Overall height: 46.7″ coupe, 46.4″ convertible. Maximum speed: L98 — 150+mph. (LT5 — 180mph. est.) Fuel consumption: 16-25mpg.

Left: part of the control panel which relies on computerized circuitry these days. The high fashion wheel (below) is good looking and functional. Facing page top: the handsome rear is marred by the absence of amber turn signals – a safety feature that should be standard throughout the industry. The big Tuned Port injected V8 (facing page bottom) will propel Corvette to almost three times the legal highway speeds.

up too much speed. First to sixth and only 50 mph. The tach reads a little under 1,500 rpm. That this car can be docile shows its versatility; later at a private airport, starting from zero, I had the car close to 100 mph in sixth gear (which is really an overdrive) by the time I ran out of runway. Of course I had switched the key over to "full" to take advantage to the engine's maximum 380 bhp. Not having the right equipment or anyone with a stopwatch, I was unable to check the car's 0-60 time, but all the magazines quote a figure of between 4.2 and 4.5 seconds. Mashing through the gears and accelerating all the way, it seems only a blink of an eye and you're there.

Cornering is phenomenal, truly phenomenal. I drove into corners at 65, 70, even 75 mph; corners I wouldn't normally consider safe at any speed above 30. An extreme right-hand bend was more tricky but the car stayed its course, helped considerably by the fine, precisely controlled steering. Naturally I didn't try cornering maneuvers in the wet, but damp straight-line getaways were taken with aplomb, spray shooting every which way. Certainly Goodyear has done a fine job with its Gatorbacks, putting that company into the top rank of tire technology.

One complaint. A problem that mars one of the finest cars ever made and a problem that is quite inexcusable in this day and age. Quality control. My test car was a 1990 model finished in bright red paint. I have already mentioned the A-pillar covers – these ought to be changed for better materials devoid of unslightly screws. The rest of the interior was quite good, apart from one or two loose threads hanging from the fabric-covered portion of the dash.

If one buys a $60,000 Mercedes there are absolutely no signs of lackluster quality. All the doors fit as they should, everything matches up perfectly. Not so on the $60,000 ZR-1. There is a real problem of fit where the hood meets the A-pillars and leading edge of the doors. On one side the gap was so large I was able to push my finger through it, and the driver's door was not flush with the hood. Paint was poorly applied and on my example was rubbing off where the roof meets the top of the C-pillar. Maybe the fiberglass mold was tired if the wavy lines in the panels were anything to go by.

A car collector friend had bought himself a 1990 ZR-1. The finish was even worse than my test example. The gaps round the hood were terrible, so sloppy was the fit; and the black paint looked as if it had been applied with one of those cheap home spray kits.

We have come to the end of our story and there is little else to say –apart from the fact that normal 1990 Corvettes are virtually unchanged from 1989. There is a new braking system called Bosch ABS II, the same as on the ZR-1. This new anti-lock braking system allows the driver complete control under sudden or heavy braking. Total swept area of the 12.9-inch vented discs is 407 square inches.

What is to come? There is already talk of a new model not far down the road – the current one is almost seven years old. As things stand at the moment there is very little that can be done to improve what is already a world-class car; unless Chevrolet decide to go mid-engine. A great plus would be for Corvette to go racing. Now GM have Lotus, a company that has more racing in its veins than anything else, there could be a wonderful tie-up between Chevrolet and themselves. There already has been with the 32-valve V-8, so let's see the Stars and Stripes back in action on the racing tracks of the world.

Apart from the quality problems that Chevrolet needs desperately to iron out, the Corvette is everything it is claimed to be. Britain's normally anti-American *Autocar/ Motor* magazine hailed the ZR-1's chassis as one of the

very best in the world; *Autoweek* claimed "…the level of handling is inspiring…." And so on it goes. Although $60,000 is an incredibly high price, the ZR-1 is a bargain compared to the Ferrari Testarossa at $134,000 and the Lamborghini Countach at $140,000.

Always appealing, always fun, the Corvette has become world class with a capital W. Chevrolet should be thanked for having the patience and fortitude not to let the Corvette go. Then there are all those great men behind it to be remembered; men who gave the Corvette its thoroughbred nature: Cole, Duntov, Earl, McLellan and Mitchell, not forgetting all the designers and engineers who helped create America's only sports car.

The ultimate Corvette – perhaps the ultimate sportscar – the 190 mph ZR-1. It is generally agreed that the ZR-1 possesses the best handling characteristics of any sports car in the world. Unfortunately, to achieve this there have been compromises, such as the inferior ride comfort, which borders on the crude and unacceptable in a world-class machine such as this. An attempt at doing something about this is evidenced by the control knob at the base of the shift lever (above). A rear view of the car (facing page top) clearly shows the difference between the ZR-1 and a standard Corvette. Facing page bottom: plastic comes in one grade whether it be on a $10,000 vehicle or in a $60,000 car such as the ZR-1. Compared to its European rivals the ZR-1 is a bargain and, all things considered, the best that money can buy.

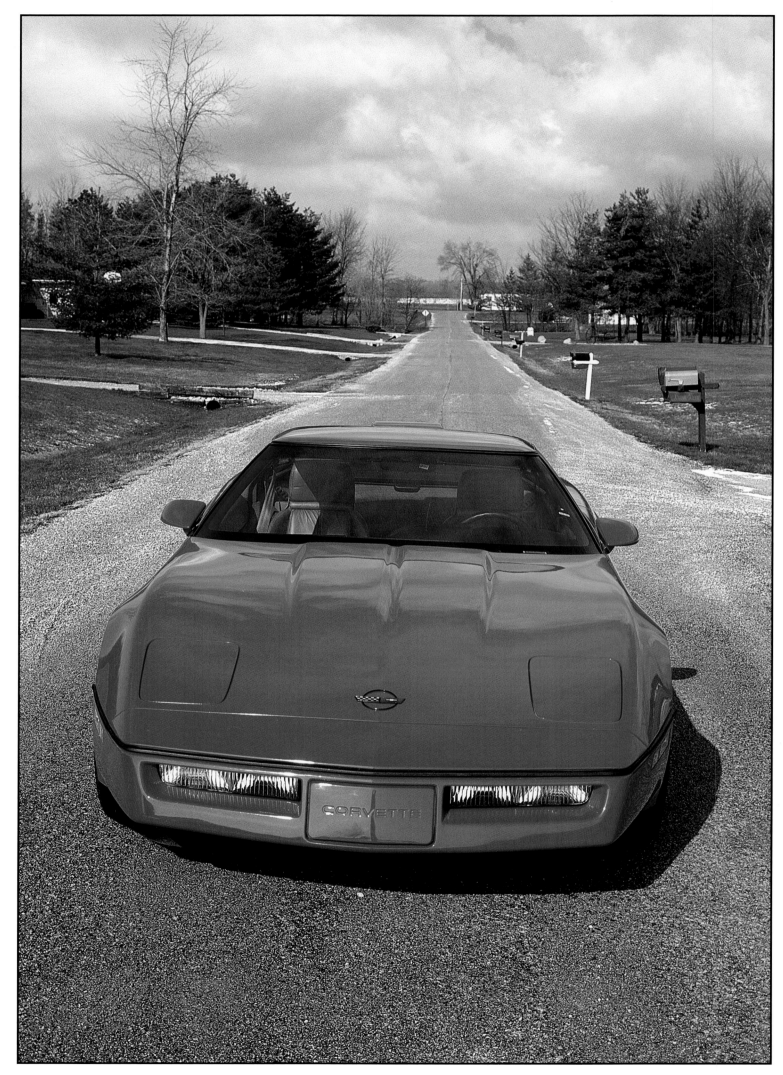